KW-223-880

Contents

SECTION 3
Evaluating different groups of tourists

SECTION 4
The economic impact

Acknowledgements

Nobody simply sits down and writes a book of this kind. Much more time is spent gathering and checking and classifying the material than working at the keyboard. Nobody can do it alone. The number of people who helped would fill a few pages and it is not possible to list them all. But they have my thanks. Some I need to give special thanks: first my wife Janet, who did much of the research; also Alan Featherby (Radisson Hotels), Peter Watson (Jetset Tours), Don Richter (Tourism Victoria), Gard Hollander (Bureau of Industry Research), Mary Barr (Department of Tourism), John Skeme (Bureau of Tourism Research), Peter Barnes (SITA), Michael Cottee (Qantas), Stan Fleetwood (Australian Bureau of Statistics), Maggie White (Australian Tourist Commission) and Robin Amos (Australian Services Union). I was always encouraged by Professor John Rickard, Pro-Vice-Chancellor and Dean of the Faculty of Business and Economics, Monash University, and appreciated the interest of Ian Kennedy, Vice President–Pacific, Pacific Asia Travel Association. I am grateful to Frances Wade for her patient and ever-caring work as an editor.

Preface

This book is a study of the economic consequences of Australian travel and tourism in the context of people movement in all its forms: inbound, outbound and domestic. It is set out in six sections.

Section 1 introduces the scale of the subject, the difficulties caused by the composition of the industry and Australia's problem in balancing the provision of facilities with tourism demand. It discusses the gathering of statistics from a scattered industry and also defines the terminology necessary for understanding the rest of the book, particularly the visitor concept and what is becoming the universally accepted definition of a tourist.

Section 2 looks in detail at where people travel in the world, with particular focus on the East Asia and Pacific Region where Australia is located, and finally on where Australians travel.

Section 3 is concerned with the money the travellers spend; it measures the expenditure of national groups, Australians in particular, as well as how much is spent by people who travel for specific purposes, from convention delegates to backpackers to Olympic Games spectators. Not all tourists have the same economic value.

Section 4 examines the economic impact in Australia of travel and tourism: on the economy as a whole, on other industries, on the balance of payments, taxation and employment, and how it affects States, Territories and particular regions. It also discusses the methodologies used for evaluating the economic impact of travel and tourism.

Section 5 considers investment—a difficult subject in most countries because of the enormous sums involved, but particularly in Australia in the 1990s when Japanese investors and Australian institutions remember only too well the losses that followed the excesses of the 1980s. This section gives examples of the investment needs of the main industry sectors and examines sources of funds and new moves to give investors confidence.

Section 6 looks to the future: the challenges in providing the accommodation needed to meet expected tourism demand, the role of the Tourism Forecasting Council and the need for reform in Commonwealth Government organisations and the introduction of planning procedures.

Readers interested in sources for attributed material will find them in the notes at the end of each section. There are few books among them because few books have been written about Australian travel and tourism. Therefore there is no bibliography. However, extensive use has been made of press references, official reports, industry publications from many sources and interviews with individuals engaged in a variety of occupations, all of which have something to do with this sometimes puzzling but always intriguing industry.

Setting the scene

The world's biggest business

TOPICS

- The economic magnitude of the industry
- Big Picture versus Enterprise View
- Australian problems
- Non-economic issues
- Definitions: 'tourist'; 'travel and tourism industry'; 'directly and indirectly'
- Industry associations
- Statistics

CHAPTER	1

Travel and tourism the Australian way

ABOUT THIS CHAPTER

Properly organised, travel and tourism can make a very large contribution to the well-being of the nation. Australians have long been enthusiastic participants in this industry and these days are being educated to understand its economic benefits. As a business, it is complex because of the huge number of companies involved and their differences in size and operation. Nevertheless, travel and tourism can respond to national strategies.

A powerful economic force

Travel and tourism is a business which embraces the world and is a powerful economic force in human affairs. It changes the fate of nations.

> Tourism . . . is on the frontline of the struggle to alleviate poverty, create jobs, increase foreign earnings, solve rural problems, and stimulate social and cultural development in the local community.

These were the words of the Secretary-General of the World Tourism Organization (WTO), Antonio Enriquez Savignac, on the occasion of an official visit to WTO headquarters in Madrid in April 1994 by the Secretary-General of the United Nations, Boutros Boutros-Ghali. The WTO is an intergovernmental agency linked to the United Nations.[1]

The paragraph, quoted from Mr Enriquez' welcoming speech, is not strikingly original but it does sum up in a few words the importance tourism is now given in world economics. It is the world's biggest business and, according to the World Travel & Tourism Council (WTTC),[2] in the year Mr Enriquez gave his succinct version of tourism's mission, it was generating annual revenues of $US3.4 trillion dollars and directly or indirectly providing one out of every nine jobs throughout the world.[3]

Australians have long contributed to this phenomenon. They are inveterate travellers, both overseas and within Australia, spending about $40 billion a year on travel and tourism in the 1990s. They spend more on tourism and travel within Australia alone than they spend in supermarkets.[4] It is only in recent times, however, that the population at large has been informed that it is playing a role in a vast business. Tourism? It means holidays, fun, travel, seeing things. It may have some educational value, but business, jobs, foreign exchange? Who would have thought it?

A few Australians did think seriously about it, years ago, before long-distance aircraft brought Australia into the world of mass travel. What they were thinking of was encouraging people from other countries to make the long, slow trip to Australia.

> I appreciate the privilege of addressing members of the chambers of commerce on an important and far-reaching proposal to advertise Australia overseas with the object of attracting investors, investor-settlers and tourists, thereby not only stimulating the more rapid development of the Commonwealth but creating new sources of revenue.

This was said in 1928 by Charles Holmes, Chairman of the Betterment & Publicity Board of the Victorian Railways, beginning an address to the Associated Chambers of Commerce of Australia at its annual conference in Hobart in February of that year. At the time Australia was attracting 20 000 visitors a year, or about as many as came in two-and-a-half days in 1993.

Despite the then esoteric nature of his subject, Mr Holmes commanded attention. Tall and distinguished-looking, he had won the Military Cross in the First World War. In the 1920s he had travelled Australia by tram, car and even camel preaching the potential and virtues of tourism.

He succeeded. As a result of the meeting in Hobart, the Australian National Travel Association (ANTA), the precursor of both the Australian Tourist Commission (ATC) and the Tourism Council Australia (TCA), was formed in 1929 and in the same year the first overseas manager left by ship to open an office in London. By 1938 there were offices in San Francisco, Wellington and Bombay as well.[5] Maybe those who had the vision to promote Australia overseas so long ago also had the vision to think that by the end of the century Australia could attract five or six million visitors a year.

Maybe it can. Forecasts for overseas visitors for the year 2000 range between 4.62 million and 6.82 million,[6] with total expenditure (including domestic tourism) between $35 billion and $44 billion (at 1992 prices) and export earnings between $15 billion and $21 billion (again at 1992 prices). The number of people employed is expected to be in the range of 600 000 to 700 000.[7]

A hundred thousand businesses

We talk in aggregate numbers, as if Australian travel and tourism were a single big company with outbound, inbound and domestic divisions. But it is not really like that. Those aggregates so carefully gathered by statisticians are the fruit of countless efforts by myriad interests, each with its own objectives; more than 100 000 businesses are involved in travel and tourism in Australia alone.[8]

The industry is made up of sectors (transport, accommodation, attractions and so on) and within most sectors, certainly the major ones, there is a great diversity in size of businesses. Qantas Airways has 27 800 people working for it, but there is only one Qantas. Even Ansett Airlines employs considerably less than half that number. Nearly twice as many people are involved in road passenger services in Australia as in air transport, but the average number of people employed by the 2825 companies affiliated with the Australian Bus and Coach Association is seven.

Big hotels employ hundreds of staff each, small ones just a few. In fact, 2.8 per cent of the three-to-five-star hotels employ one-third of the category workforce. Half the hotels in that range are three-star and they employ an average of 11 each. There are thousands of accommodation establishments which do not rate as three-star and employ fewer than that.

What of attractions? Heritage organisations attract visitors. Of the 48 200 people who work for them, 42 300 are not even paid![9]

Because of the dissimilarity of businesses involved in travel and tourism, it is not easy to make generalised judgements about their costs or profit potential, to assess employment opportunities or to devise training programs.

The Big Picture

Yet we can deal with the impact of travel and tourism on the Australian economy; we can put measurements on tourism activity and determine what it costs to make it work and expand it. We can do this if we take the Big Picture perspective on travel and tourism, the national view, the view of governments and their promotional agencies, researchers, planners, economists and academics. These people measure the progress of tourism and trace its impact on the Australian economy. For this purpose, they treat it as if it were one business.

The Enterprise View

The Enterprise View is the other way of looking at travel and tourism. This is how the people working in the industry see it, and most of them are in the private sector. The Big Picture may tell a story of progress and prosperity, travel movements going up, national revenue increasing and so on, but it may or may not have immediate meaning for them: they may or may not be sharing in that prosperity. Their only valid measurement is the bottom line on their own profit-and-loss statements, which tells whether or not their businesses will survive and prosper or whether they will fail and disappear.

It is not surprising that the Big Picture outlook and the Enterprise View are not always in harmony.

> I don't think anyone is arguing that overseas visitor numbers won't double this decade. Everyone in tourism has been talking about these big gross numbers: numbers of tourists, numbers of rooms, numbers of flights. But hardly anyone has been talking about the most important number: the bottom line. The only way Australian tourism can attract investment dollars from local funds and banks or overseas is to show a comparable bottom line with similar safe tourism destinations, such as Hawaii, Saipan and Singapore.[10]

In 1992, the Commonwealth Minister for Tourism attempted to explain to an audience of 400 motel owners and managers his Government's national strategy document which called for up to 90 000 new first-class bedrooms to be built by the year 2000 to meet forecast demand—a new hotel a week for eight years, as he put it. At the time Australia was in recession and the motel executives, beset by low occupancies and low yields, were concerned about what was going to happen next week, not next century. Nor did they see the Department of the Treasury and the banks as their natural allies. The Minister's comments 'sparked one of the rowdiest sessions ever at an industry conference'.[11]

While the choice of time and audience might not have been the best for such a discussion to be harmonious, perhaps in the long run it led to better understanding. Both sides do need to understand each other's position; both are essential to advancing Australia's prosperity through travel and tourism.

Directing travel and tourism

The common factor driving all the travel and tourism businesses, big and small, is their response to tourism demand: in other words, the desire or need to travel that is implanted in much of the world's population.

The system that has evolved can be likened to a complex blood vessels: great arteries linking organs and wispy capillaᵣ access to remote parts of the body. The motivation to travel keeᵣ circulating and there are experts galore monitoring it, prescribing cures toɪ its ills and potions to increase its flow. But does the beast the system serves have a brain?

Does it need one? Does not each of those 100 000-plus businesses do its own planning and respond to whatever happens, good or bad? Is this not a classic case of market forces at work? Is tourism not as fickle as fashion? How can you have a central control?

You cannot have, and do not want to have, a central control in Australia, but it has been proven in this country that tourism can be directed by marketing and the provision of facilities, and so can respond to national and regional strategies.[12]

National programs to encourage tourism are relatively recent, with few reaching back to the start of the twentieth century.

> At first, the approach was one-sided: to promote what existed. Then, but still far too slowly, national agencies began to broaden their programs to encompass both sides of the marketing equation: demand and supply. And a new philosophy emerged: to apply to this scattered industry *modern marketing research* and then *planning*—to balance promotion and plant capacity and to project both programs five or ten years or more into the future.[13]

Australia has been unsuccessful in balancing plant capacity and demand. At the national level we seem to have been obsessed with overseas visitor demand; the Australian Tourist Commission has been spending far more on promotion per tourist arrival than any other national tourist organisation.[14] Yet it is only in the 1990s that the Commonwealth Government has taken its first definite steps towards encouraging the supply side, by providing better information for investors.

Workable planning links have not been established between the Commonwealth, the States and Territories and the tourism regions and, to make matters worse, the Commonwealth Government has incomprehensibly split responsibilities between its own agencies.[15] Although industry organisations have improved their status and their lobbying performance in recent years, they have not been able to concentrate enough influence to bring about change. Indeed, it is doubtful if the consultative mechanisms in place can be effective.

The formation of a new body, the Tourism Council Australia, to replace the Australian Tourism Industry Association in December 1994 is a recognition of difficulties encountered in industry representation.[16]

Section 5 of this book ('Investment,' pages 123–50) deals with one of the consequences of inadequate tourism planning: the aftermath of the building boom of the 1980s, the losses, the sell-offs to foreign investors and the distaste the big Australian investors, the financial institutions, have for tourism projects, particularly accommodation projects. The attitude of leading financiers was illustrated in October 1991, when a function was held to bring together government and financial officials to discuss problems associated with investment in tourism plant.

> No banks or [financial] institutions attended. One finance company executive said his organisation was not willing to spend $68 to attend the seminar because 'it wasn't willing to invest this much on tourism.'[17]

Reality starts at the local level

The establishment of a Tourism Forecasting Council, with an impressive representation of Australian industry and authorities, may be the beginning of the answer to a problem that becomes more serious as tourism increases. The role of this body is to provide tourism-related industries with realistic and relevant tourism forecasts—not only broad national forecasts, but also specific regional ones.

It is important to think in regional terms. It is not only governments and big companies that shape our future in the world's biggest industry. In the long run, the collective view from the regions will be more important than that from Canberra because the real challenge of national planning, if one day we choose to indulge in it, is to convert the Big Picture view to micro-economic reality at a local level. What is needed in tourism plant, attractions and facilities must be determined at the local level first; as a consequence, planning has to work upwards, not downwards.

Australia has already paid a high price for not getting its travel and tourism institutions and their functions right. That is not the subject of this book, however, although its economic consequences are taken note of here.

This book sets out the economic framework; anybody involved in travel and tourism (or intends to become involved in even the smallest enterprise associated with it) needs knowledge of the environment in which he or she operates. In travel and tourism, it is usually what is happening beyond the far horizons which affects the bottom line.

Other issues

What of the romance of travel, the wonderful holidays by the sea or in the mountains, the visits to faraway places, the dreamy tropical nights with the stars hanging bright in the heavens? Many people have a romantic view of it. Tourism also can be thought of as thrilling, fun, educational, life-seeing, even life-fulfilling. Some see it as having social and political benefits brought about by the traveller's exposure to different peoples and cultures.

In considering the subject-matter of this book, we must recognise that whatever else they say about travel and tourism, the governments, companies and people who make it work are in it for the money. Economists measure its net worth to a nation or community; that is, the result of what it earns and what it costs.

The positive economic aspects of travel and tourism, expressed in big numbers, are often mentioned. Sometimes the numbers bewilder as much as they inform. But in some economies size or rapid growth can be a disadvantage, drawing off resources, such as labour, that might be used better in other ways—and thus increasing costs throughout the economy. 'Leakage' must be considered—the proportion of what tourists spend that is paid for imports. This is not just what tourists spend in buying an imported Italian scarf or a souvenir made in Korea. There are more subtle forms of leakage. For example, Qantas Airways having aircraft serviced overseas may be sound business for Qantas, but it also has its impact on the national accounts.

Tourism can have negative impacts on other valuable industries. Studies discussed in Chapter 8 have shown that an increase in international tourism into Australia can adversely affect mining and agricultural exports. This contributes to surprising results when we assess the net worth of inbound tourism to the individual States; for example, Queensland does not benefit to the extent that might be expected from tourism growth, partly because its economy is also heavily dependent on agricultural and mining exports.

Tourism becomes a major factor in government economic strategies, in containing costs and negative impacts on other industries, in encouraging national saving to pay for necessary imports of equipment to service increasing demand, and so on. There is no question that Australia benefits economically from travel and tourism, but the agreeable prospect of big numbers getting bigger should not mask the total effect on the Australian economy— the negative factors as well as the positive—and, for governments, the responsibility to devise strategies to achieve the best benefits for communities and the nation as a whole.

There are costs (and benefits) which do not fit into annual financial statements. The real test of travel and tourism is not just its economic impact, but also its total effect on the well-being of a nation or a community. This is rather more difficult to measure than just the economic matters, but all the issues that affect it should be considered.

'A school for dignity'

We began by quoting the Secretary-General of the World Tourism Organization, who put forward the positive side of tourism: it could help alleviate poverty, create jobs, increase foreign earnings, solve rural problems and stimulate social and cultural development. In reply, the Secretary-General of the United Nations acknowledged the positive impact of tourism on economic and social development, but also raised the subject of tourism ethics.

> A genuine tourism ethic is in effect necessary and it is incumbent on the World Tourism Organization to articulate and implement that ethic. The dangers of unbridled tourism, of a tourism that fails to respect the places visited or the communities encountered are well known. Tourism must be a school for dignity. For it is absolutely essential to prevent it from altering too profoundly the nature of sites and the lifestyles of host populations. We are all aware that tourism transforms local mentalities and introduces new concepts of work, monetary value and inter-personal relations.
>
>   Consequently, to ensure that tourism does not lead to a loss of cultural identity, it must be well thought out by States and by people on a universal scale.[18]

People who make their living from travel and tourism are concerned that their resources—the coastlines, mountainsides, forests and historic buildings—are not degraded or destroyed. Once they are gone they cannot be reclaimed.

> But what has tourism done to the Mediterranean? And what is it doing to those further flung places like the Caribbean? What has it done to Bali?
>
>   First and foremost it has brought wealth. Spain has advanced economically and politically eighty years in the space of twenty. What was in the 60s a rather economically backward country ruled by a dictator and with a peasant agriculture, is now a prosperous, stylish industrialized democracy. More expensive too, which is another motivation for tourists to gravitate towards poorer and cheaper countries on different continents.
>
>   But tourism has done other things as well. The Mediterranean at the moment sees about 120 million visitors a year, about a quarter of all tourists. By the year 2000 the number of international tourist arrivals will probably have risen to 200 million. But the Mediterranean, arguably the most beautiful, is probably the dirtiest sea in the world. Not wholly as a result of tourism development—industrial effluent is responsible for much of the pollution. Mediterranean shores are also the most built-up. American astronauts said that from space the coasts of Spain, France, Italy and parts of Greece looked like a continuous village.[19]

Money is not everything. This book is concerned with economics, not the social and environmental issues of tourism; but in the final summing-up, all are entries in the same set of accounts.

CHAPTER 2

Defining, organising, measuring

ABOUT THIS CHAPTER

Words have different meanings for different people. To measure the effects of travel and tourism, some precise definitions have to be agreed upon and some jargon accepted. The essential terminology—what is meant by 'tourism', 'travel and tourism', the 'industry' and 'directly and indirectly'—is dealt with in this chapter, as well as the role of industry associations. The use of statistics to assess different aspects of the industry is also discussed.

What is a tourist?

Tourism has been around a long time. A Greek called Herodotus, who lived in the fifth century BC, is sometimes called the first tourist. It is doubtful if he were, but he is the first we know of who travelled widely to satisfy his own curiosity and he left a very readable account of his wanderings. One of his 'life-seeing' observations was of a birthday party in Persia, where pickled duck and barley wine were served and the host circulated with the replica of a corpse, 'to encourage his guests to reflect upon mortality'.

It might be said that he is the first tourist on record.[20] Keeping records, or statistics, of tourists—noting where they go, what they see and do, what they spend and so on—is an essential part of the business of travel and tourism.

Statistics are only really useful if they are collected according to standard definitions; otherwise one set of figures cannot be compared with another. What is there to measure? What are we trying to define? What is tourism?

The *Concise Oxford Dictionary* gives the word 'tourism' as a noun of French derivation meaning 'organized touring; operation of tours as a business; provision of things and services that attract tourists'. A tourist is a 'person who makes a tour, traveller, esp. for recreation'.

That is not good enough for the statisticians, who in their efforts to be precise have given us any number of definitions. The World Tourism Organization defines tourism as 'the activities of persons travelling to and staying in places outside their usual environment for not more than one consecutive year for leisure, business and other purposes'.[21]

It is the definition of a 'tourist' that has caused the biggest problem — the problem being that a number of definitions have been devised to meet particular purposes. The 1986 Australian Government Inquiry into Tourism examined quite a few and settled on one used previously by the Bureau of Industry Economics:

> Specifically, a tourist is defined as either:
> - a person who undertakes travel, for any reason, involving a stay away from his or her usual place of residence for at least one night; or
> - a person who undertakes a pleasure trip involving a stay away from home for at least four hours during daylight, and involving a round trip distance of at least 50 km; however, for trips to national parks, state and forest reserves, museums, historical parks, animal parks and other man-made attractions, the distance limitation does not apply.[22]

The definition used for the Domestic Tourism Monitor, which charts the travel movements of Australians within Australia, defines a tourist as one who travels at least 40 kilometres from home and stays away at least one night.

The last word

What should be the last word on the subject in this country comes from the Australian Bureau of Statistics (ABS), which has produced a *Framework for the Collection and Publication of Tourism Statistics* in an attempt to bring about a unity of approach by statistics collectors. The ABS approach is consistent with WTO and United Nations Statistical Office recommendations on tourism statistics.

The Bureau specifies separate definitions for 'international visitor' and 'domestic visitor' because separate data are needed for each category. The definitions are:

> *International visitor:* A person arriving in a country who
>   (i) normally resides outside that country,
>   (ii) is visiting for a period of less than 12 months, and
>   (iii) is not visiting for the purpose of taking up work remunerated from within the country visited.
>
> *Domestic visitor:* A person making a trip within a country who
>   (i) normally resides in that country, but is visiting a place outside his/her usual environment,

(ii) is visiting a destination for a period of less than 12 months, and

(iii) is not visiting for the purpose of taking up work remunerated from within the place visited.

Note is taken that some domestic definitions, like the Domestic Tourism Monitor, use a more specific cut-off of 40 kilometres beyond which a person must travel to be defined as a visitor. This is valid:

> . . . where it is consistent with 'usual environment'. An example of where it would *not* be consistent is where travel to a place more than 40 kms away is undertaken *within the same city*. Travel within a person's usual city of residence should be regarded as within the 'usual environment'.[23]

So a tourist is a visitor who travels for any reason other than to work and be paid from within the area he or she visits. The holiday traveller, business person and convention delegate are all tourists, as are those people who travel to see friends or relatives, to undergo health treatment or who embark on religious pilgrimages.

> All types of travellers engaged in tourism are described as visitors. Therefore the term 'visitor' represents the basic concept for the whole system of tourism statistics.[24]

Travel and tourism

Some people prefer to be thought of as travellers rather than tourists. A writer in *The Sunday Age* suggested that the intelligent 'traveller' be a 'tourist-avoider'. In particular he advised avoidance of the 'masses of swirling, multilingual hordes armed with guide books, video cameras and egomaniacal "attitude"' who were turning Florence into 'little more than a "Renaisso-Disneyland"'.[25] The World Wide Fund for Nature produces a range of local and overseas tour programs described as 'adventures of the mind' for 'travellers not tourists'.

But the statisticians do not distinguish between the two. At one time it was usual to say that 'travel' and 'tourism' were interchangeable in statistical terms; now it is common to join the two together to make the point. There are word linkages in use like 'tourism and leisure' and 'travel and hospitality', but 'travel and tourism' has become the accepted form for the all-embracing term that describes the collection of businesses engaged in satisfying tourism demand. It is used by the World Tourism Organization and forms part of the name of the World Travel & Tourism Council (WTTC).

The travel and tourism industry

The term 'travel and tourism' is also used in 'travel and tourism industry', just as the terms 'travel industry' and 'tourism industry' are also used, often (but not always) with the same intended meaning.

Travel and tourism is not classified as an industry: an industry is defined by the Australian Bureau of Statistics[26] as a group of businesses or enterprises that carry out similar economic activities. Australia's new standard industry classification, called 'the Australian and New Zealand Standard Industry Classification' (ANZSIC) because it is a joint affair with New Zealand, has been developed for use in the production of industrial statistics. It breaks the economy into 465 industries and, because it is a new classification, recognises the importance of service industries. Tourism is not among them.

> Travel or tourism is essentially a market or demand force rather than an industry. There are many separate trades and a wide range of interests. It is the demand aspect which gives the trade its unity and identity.[27]

It has been called a 'trade', but these days the term 'industry' is used to describe that collection of 'many separate trades' and 'wide range of interests', whether or not it fits the standard definition. It will continue to be used.

Directly involved organisations

Businesses

'Travel and tourism industry' is a term generally used to denote those businesses which are *directly* concerned with travel and tourism. Here are some examples:[28]

Travel
Travel companies:
airlines
coach companies
railways
rent-a-cars
cruise-ship lines

Travel services:
travel agencies
tour operators
duty-free shops
convention organisers
incentive travel houses.

Hospitality
Accommodation:
hotels
motels
resorts
caravan parks

Food and beverage:
restaurants
bars and cafés
catering companies
function centres.

Attractions

Year-round:	*Events:*
natural	festivals
animal parks	sporting events
museums/galleries	theatrical events
theme parks	cultural events.

Government organisations

The Commonwealth Government has a number of organisations directly involved in tourism, including the Department of Tourism, the Australian Tourist Commission, the Bureau of Tourism Research and the Tourism Forecasting Council. Each State and Territory has a promotional organisation—most of them, like the Australian Tourist Commission, statutory authorities. Additionally, many of the people who work at attractions such as national parks, museums and galleries, or at information centres, are employees of government organisations.

Indirectly involved organisations

Companies which construct or manufacture travel and tourism buildings and equipment—like hotels, motels, coaches, aircraft or boats—and which supply food and beverages, are said to be *indirectly* involved in travel and tourism. They include people and companies who may not think of themselves as being involved, from the butcher who supplies the local motel with meat to Aerospace Technologies of Australia and Hawker de Havilland, Australian companies that make parts for Boeing 747 aircraft.[29]

Industry associations

Industry associations play an important part in their various sectors and in the co-ordination between the sectors. Most represent small businesses (not necessarily exclusively) which alone would not have a voice. Associations present their members' interests to governments, advise on such matters as the law and industrial relations, set standards and assist with training. Some carry out a research function and may also provide forums for industry discussion.

The Tourism Council Australia (TCA) which, as has been noted, had its origins in the formation of the Australian National Travel Association in 1929, is the umbrella body, representing to government the needs and views of the industry as a whole. It stages the Australian Tourism Conference each year at which the national tourism awards are announced. It also provides the secretariat for regular 'CEOs' meetings' at which chief executives of a representative group of sector associations meet to discuss common issues. Previously known as the Australian Tourism Industry Association (ATIA), it was reorganised as the Tourism Council Australia at the end of 1994, aiming for a wider membership and a more effective voice for the industry.[30]

The following list is an indication of the number and variety of associations whose members are involved in tourism:

Association of Australian Convention Bureaux
Association of Convention Executives
Australian Automobile Association
Australian Bus and Coach Association
Australian Council of Tour Wholesalers
Australian Duty Free Operators' Association
Australian Federation of Travel Agents
Australian Hotels Association
Australian Incentive Association
Australian Institute of Travel & Tourism Inc.
Australian Society of Association Executives
Board of Airline Representatives of Australia
Caravan and Camping Industry Association
Exhibition Industry Association of Australia
Hotel Sales and Marketing Association
Inbound Tourism Organisation of Australia Ltd
Meetings Industry Association of Australia
Motor Inn, Motel and Accommodation Association
National Restaurant and Catering Association
Retail Traders Association
Society of Incentive Travel Executives
Tourism Task Force.

A note on statistics

This book relies on statistics; it could not have been written if there were not constant collections of data in Australia and studies and analyses of many different kinds. Without them, there would be no basis for judging the worth of travel and tourism, no real knowledge of trends, no sound basis for further investment. However, it is also necessary to understand the limitations of statistics. The picture they present is still incomplete; there are time lags and imperfections because of sampling problems.

We have already seen that tourism is not included in the Australian industry classification system; it is an activity that cuts across a number of industry groupings rather than fitting neatly into its own. Internationally, a new statistical approach, Standard Industry Classification of Tourism Activity (SICTA) has been devised. This picks out the categories of business which are important to travel and tourism and collects the numbers—even in businesses of which some part is related to tourism and some not. The Australian Bureau of Statistics is examining the new system with a view to adopting it in Australia.

At this time, it is not possible to accurately assess in detail all of the desirable information about the industry or its sectors. Labour statistics will serve as an example of why this is so. The ABS publishes its monthly Catalogue No. 6203.0, *The Labour Force, Australia*, which gives figures for the following industry divisions:

agriculture, forestry, fishing and
  hunting
mining
manufacturing
electricity, gas and water
construction
wholesale and retail trade
transport and storage

communication
finance, property and business
  services
public administration and
  defence
community services
recreation, personal and other
  services.

These are further broken down into subdivisions, but those precisely identifiable with travel and tourism are only the transport categories (and some of these include freight services) and 'restaurants, hotels and clubs' in the 'recreational, personal and other services' division.

Census figures are another source of labour statistics, but in the reporting of the 1991 Census, much of the detail previously available in print has not been issued in that form, though it is said to be available on CD-ROM. However, this information is difficult, if not impossible, to access through the library system.

The ABS has issued detailed studies of amusement and theme parks, the hospitality industry and the motor vehicle hire industry, all for the 1991–92 year and all based on separate surveys. These were published in 1994.

There has also been a considerable time-lag in the overall employment figures issued by the Bureau of Tourism Research. The Commonwealth Department of Tourism includes these in *Impact*, its invaluable monthly fact sheet on the economic impact of tourism and the latest visitor arrival trends. The November 1994 *Impact* carried a figure of 466 700 employed directly or indirectly to tourism in 1991–92. However, by late 1994 a new input–output study, which will provide information for an updated analysis, was nearing completion. This study will also provide new material for estimating tourism's contribution to Gross Domestic Product and the total expenditure derived from tourism.

New studies are needed from time to time, not only to provide current estimates but also to update the methodology. For example, the number and types of businesses benefiting indirectly from tourism are bound to change as tourism expands. Some key ratios still in use—the estimate of the proportion of imports in tourism spending, for instance—date back to Bureau of Industry Economics work of the early 1980s.

Methodology affects accuracy. We have an example in Chapter 12 (pages 104–5) in which ABS figures for employment in the air transport sector are several thousand fewer than the aggregate of the two biggest companies, Qantas Airways and Ansett Airlines. The reason for this is that the ABS figures are derived from household surveys and some people responding do not know or do not declare themselves to be employed in air transport. They may simply see themselves as office cleaners, for instance.

The two great surveys that track travel and tourism in Australia each year are the International Visitor Survey and the Domestic Tourism Monitor.

- The International Visitor Survey is based on 12 000 interviews conducted at airports as international visitors leave Australia. Data from the survey are used to provide visitor arrivals, visitor profiles, travel arrangements, airlines used, and detailed coverage of trip itineraries, including expenditure.
- The Domestic Tourism Monitor is derived from information on domestic travel behaviour collected in interviews with 65 000 people; in 1993–94 detailed information was collected on about 15 000 trips involving an overnight stay. Day-trip information has been included since the 1988–89 survey and expenditure information since 1993–94.

It should be noted that the International Visitor Survey is conducted with people 15 years old and over and the Domestic Tourism Monitor with people 14 years old and over. The ABS arrival and departure figures are for all people, regardless of age.

The purpose of this note is not to denigrate the collection and analysis of travel and tourism statistics in Australia or to deprecate their value. It is an enormous task, often difficult and usually expensive. We are fortunate that we have available so much information to guide us and that there are constant improvements in the quality and range of that information. But we should know what the statistics truly represent so that we make the best use of them.

To return to the example of the air transport figures in Chapter 12: we were content to use both sets of figures because, while the ABS numbers were undoubtedly understated, they were compatible with the figures for other transport modes derived from the same sampling method and therefore comparisons of employment levels could be made with confidence.

What we want from statistics is scale, relationships and trends; last-digit accuracy is of no consequence.

NOTES ON SECTION 1

1   Australia is not a member. It withdrew from the world body in July 1990, although the Department of Tourism says it still exchanges pertinent information. Mr Enriquez' speech was reported in *WTO News*, No. 3, May/June 1994, p. 1.

2   While the WTO is the official world body to which governments belong (but not Australia's), the World Travel & Tourism Council is a coalition of chief executive officers from all sectors of the industry. Several Australian chief executive officers are members. The WTO is headquartered in Madrid, and the WTTC in Brussels.

3   Although travel and tourism has been the world's biggest industry for some years, it is not perceived as such by everybody. A survey conducted in 1993 for the WTTC with 475 respondents in 23 countries showed that 'policy and opinion makers' believed electronics was the biggest industry. Travel and tourism ranked fifth, in their opinion.

4   'What we spend at supermarkets now adds up to $25 billion a year', *Sunday Herald Sun*, 31 July 1994, p. 101. Australians spend about $30 billion a year within Australia on travel and tourism. See Chapter 6.

5   An extract of Mr Holmes' speech was printed in a journal for former staff members of the Australian Tourist Commission, *The Galah Gazette*, December 1993. The other information is from an article in the June 1993 issue by Basil Atkinson, the first General Manager of the Australian Tourist Commission, and before that Chief Executive of the Australian National Travel Association, having taken over that role from Mr Holmes in 1957. Mr Atkinson is one of the visionaries of the postwar era, recognised not only in Australia but on the world scene.

6   See Chapter 16. The 6.82 million figure has been called a 'target' because it was arrived at using different methodology to the other figures; in the normal sense of the word it is still a forecast.

7   *Impact*, a monthly fact sheet on the economic impact of tourism and the latest visitor arrival trends, issued by the Department of Tourism, May 1994 issue.

8   Estimate based on Bureau of Tourism Research figures for employment in the travel and tourism industry, allowance for non-small business employment and Australian Bureau of Statistics estimates of average small business employment.

9   See Table 12.11, page 112.

10 Ross Woods, Tourism Director for Horwath & Horwath, quoted in 'Why banks won't invest', *Business Review Weekly*, 14 February 1992, pp. 18–21.

11 *TravelTrade*, 2–15 September 1992, p. 36. The then Minister for Tourism, Alan Griffiths, was speaking at the Flag International Conference in Perth. 'During a hectic question time, several delegates called on Mr Griffiths to talk with Treasury regarding assistance for investment in the tourism industry. Delegates told him the banks' policies were anti-accommodation investment.' The document on which the 90 000 extra room figure was based, the Commonwealth Department of Tourism's *Tourism—Australia's Passport to Growth: A National Tourism Strategy* estimated that between 30 000 and 90 000 rooms would have to be constructed between 1992 and 2000 to meet demand, depending on which forecast was used. Press reports inevitably cited 90 000. See Chapter 16.

12 It is arguable whether anything has been proved nationally, but it has certainly been proved on a State, Territory and regional basis.

13 Dan Wallace, Director of Marketing, Canadian Government Office of Tourism, speech to the American Management Associations Conference, New York, February 1974.

14 In 1992 Australia ranked fourth in national tourist organisation promotional spending behind Spain, France and the United Kingdom, but those countries had much higher arrivals figures. The World Tourism Organization calculated that Australia spent $US19.63 per tourist arrival, France

$US1.21, Spain $US2.15 and the United Kingdom $US3.25. No other country on the WTO list came close to Australia's per tourist spending on promotion. *WTO News*, September 1994, p. 10.

15 See Chapter 17.

16 The Tourism Council Australia was announced at the Australian Tourism Conference in Adelaide on 21 September 1994.

17 *Business Review Weekly*, 14 February 1992, p. 21.

18 Boutros Boutros-Ghali, United Nations Secretary-General, reported in *WTO News*, No. 3, May/June 1994.

19 Martin Brackenbury, President of the International Federation of Tour Operators and Director of Thomson Travel Group (United Kingdom) at a Round Table on Trends and Challenges of Tourism Beyond the Year 2000, WTO 10th General Assembly, Bali, Indonesia, 30 September–9 October 1993.

20 'Herodotus' curiosity and enthusiastic enjoyment take fire at any feat of intellect or energy, or any wonderful thing away among far-off lands and peoples'—André Bonnard in *Greek Civilisation*, George Allen & Unwin Ltd, London, p. 149. The birthday party description is from *Going Places: The Ways of the Tourist from Imperial Rome to the Present Day*, by Maxine Feifer, Macmillan, London, 1985, p. 220. Herodotus wrote prolifically on a number of subjects and is known to scholars as the 'father of history'.

21 *Recommendations on Tourism Statistics*, World Tourism Organization, Madrid, 1994.

22 *Report of the Australian Government Inquiry into Tourism*, 1986, Vol. 1, p. 11.

23 *Framework for the Collection and Publication of Tourism Statistics*, June 1991, pp. 5–6.

24 *Recommendations on Tourism Statistics*, World Tourism Organization, Madrid, 1994.

25 *The Sunday Age*, 15 August 1993, Agenda 10.

26 For example, see ABS Catalogue No. 1298.0, *Introducing the Australian and New Zealand Standard Industrial Classification (ANZSIC)*.

27 L. J. Lickorish, Director-General, British Tourist Authority, in a speech, Canberra, 1979.

28 This is not a full list; for example, there are many different kinds of accommodation such as bed and breakfast, host farms etc. However, the main types of companies are listed to give a picture of the industry.

29 The Bureau of Industry Economics, in the preface to its landmark 1979 study on the economic impact of tourism, first noted that 'the term "tourism industry" is a generic expression since no such homogeneous entity exists' and then said: 'It would be illogical to exclude some existing activities from the definition merely because they supply fewer goods or services to tourists than others. The definition adopted is therefore "all activities which supply goods or services directly or indirectly to tourism final demand, the relative significance of each activity in the tourism industry being determined by the value of goods or services supplied to tourism final demand". It should be noted that this definition includes industries which supply goods and services to tourism final demand only indirectly, for example materials used in boat building.'

30 The Chairman of ATIA, Sir Frank Moore, said disunity in Australia's tourism industry had 'weakened its lobbying power with governments and its credibility among business groups and the general community'—*The Australian*, 23 September 1994, p. 5. The newspaper quoted Sir Frank Moore as saying 'ATIA's main rival', the Tourism Task Force, would be invited to join the Council and indicated that he expected all industry groups to eventually merge with the new body.

Where people travel in the world

People exchange equals money exchange

TOPICS

- How the 747 changed world travel
- Australia's place in the fastest-growing region
- Changing travel patterns: exceptional growth from some Asian markets
- Australia's share of important markets
- Home and abroad: where Australians travel
- How airline deregulation changed domestic travel habits

CHAPTER 3

The East Asia and Pacific Region

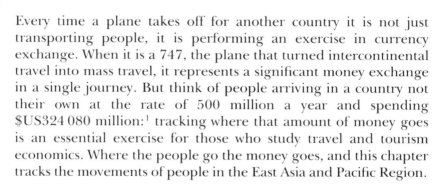

ABOUT THIS CHAPTER

Every time a plane takes off for another country it is not just transporting people, it is performing an exercise in currency exchange. When it is a 747, the plane that turned intercontinental travel into mass travel, it represents a significant money exchange in a single journey. But think of people arriving in a country not their own at the rate of 500 million a year and spending $US324 080 million:[1] tracking where that amount of money goes is an essential exercise for those who study travel and tourism economics. Where the people go the money goes, and this chapter tracks the movements of people in the East Asia and Pacific Region.

It's more than a plane

Nothing symbolises the age of mass travel so much as the jumbo jet, the Boeing 747. It first flew with paying passengers in January 1970 in the white-and-blue colours of Pan American World Airways, the airline which inspired it. Pan Am is bankrupt and no longer flying 747s (or anything else). But the 747 is the pride of the fleets of more than 80 other airlines; it is the unchallenged ruler of the skies. The Boeing Company expects to be still building 747s in the next century.

Already, more than one thousand have been built in 15 major derivatives. Some of the first 747s are still flying but the latest version, the 747-400, uses a third less fuel, flies twice as far and can carry about 100 more passengers. It has many improvements—better aerodynamics, turned-up

winglets, new avionics, a digital flight deck and the latest passenger entertainment systems. But it is still unmistakably a 747, and most of its predeces-
sors are still flying. Every hour of every day the ungainly monsters are taking
to the air somewhere in the world, transporting as many as 600 people at a
time from one part of the planet to another.

In theory, the world's 747s—they are usually fitted with between 400
and 500 seats—could be carrying nearly half a million people at any one
time. In fact, by mid-1993 they had carried more than 1.4 billion passengers,
or the equivalent of one in every four people then living. No other vehicle
in history has had such an effect on the scale of people-movement. Yet at
the time it was designed, it was not expected to have a long life as a passenger
jet. Supersonic jet transports were on the way and the 747s were designed
so they could be converted to freighters.

In the meantime, Pan Am wanted a plane to achieve a 30 per cent
reduction in transoceanic operating costs. The 747 did that. The supersonics
came and made no impact on mass travel, but the size, comfort and economics of the 747 brought about a revolution over long distances. It was a success
because, although it was a monster aircraft, the weight per seat was reduced
compared with other aircraft at that time—and so was the cost per seat.

'The jumbo jet changed the way we see our world'[2]—and the way we
spend our money. The 747s changed not only the economics of travel but
also the economies of nations. The jumbos move more than people; they are
also massive movers of money; they are a medium of exchange of wealth of
great magnitude.

Think about it. People pay to ride in them and the money is spent by
the airlines in different countries on aircraft, salaries, fuel, marketing, rents
and many other goods and services. (For example, before Qantas Airways
became a domestic as well as an international carrier half its revenue was
spent overseas.) The travellers themselves spend money in the country to
which the big planes take them—on accommodation, food, internal travel,
entrance to attractions, shopping and other things.

The Boeing 747s have not changed the world of travel all on their own;
they are by no means the only planes in the skies. Nor is the aeroplane
always the most used form of transport. Within Australia, nearly 80 per cent
of domestic travel measured by 'trips' is by private motor vehicle. But no
other vehicle has changed travel patterns like the aeroplane in recent times—
deregulation in Australia has given us another example —and the Boeing
747 has had the biggest influence so far on volume of long-distance travellers.

The fastest-growing region

It does not matter how people travel; they spend money doing it, and nearly
1.5 million people cross international borders every day. In 1993, on an
average day, they spent $US888 million.

Australia is in the fastest-growing of the six regions into which the World Tourism Organization divides the world: the East Asia and Pacific Region, a long slice of the planet with China marking its northern and western extremities, the islands of French Polynesia its eastern and Australia and New Zealand its southern. It includes the world's most populous nation, China, which is visited by about 20 million people from other countries each year; and tiny territories like Tuvalu and Yap State, which record about 1000 international visitors annually. A full list of East Asian and Pacific countries follows:[3]

North-East Asia
China
Hong Kong
Japan
South Korea
Macao
Mongolia
Taiwan

South-East Asia
Brunei
Cambodia
Indonesia
Laos
Malaysia
Philippines
Singapore
Thailand
Vietnam

Australia/New Zealand
Australia
New Zealand

Melanesia
Fiji
New Caledonia
Papua New Guinea
Solomon Islands
Vanuatu

Micronesia
Guam
Kiribati
Mariana Islands
Marshall Islands
Pohnpei State
Truk State
Yap State

Polynesia
American Samoa
Cook Islands
French Polynesia
Niue
Samoa
Tonga
Tuvalu

In 1993, the East Asia and Pacific Region recorded an 11.8 per cent increase in visitor arrivals over 1992, more than double the growth performance of any other region.

However, before we get too excited we should put our region into perspective. Measured in international arrivals, East Asia and the Pacific produced just 13.7 per cent of world tourism and Australia 0.52 per cent in 1993. On the other hand, the Mediterranean area alone attracts nearly a quarter of the world's arrivals (120 million) and Europe as a whole about three-fifths. Table 3.1 shows how the regions compared.

Table 3.1   International arrivals in world regions in 1993

Region	1993		% change 1993–92	
	Arrivals	Receipts	Arrivals	Receipts
	million	$USm	million	$USm
Africa	17.9	6 364	2.0	8.7
Americas	106.5	95 545	5.6	14.3
East Asia/Pacific	68.5	52 587	11.8	15.2
Europe	296.5	162 573	2.1	5.7
Middle East	7.2	4 996	–8.4	–7.4
South Asia	3.4	2 015	–1.4	–2.9
WORLD	500.0	324 800	3.8	9.3

Source: WTO

Motivations for travel

People travel in the world not only because they want to, but when they have the time and can afford to. Factors which affect demand for a destination include:

- incomes in source markets
- air fares to the destination
- the price of travel and tourism services at the destination
- the amount of leisure time available in the source markets (e.g. average length of holidays)
- demographic factors affecting the size of target market segments (e.g. the proportion of high-income people without dependent families, young backpackers and so on)
- promotion
- the exchange rate between the source country and the destination.

The influence of exchange rates

The weakening of the Australian dollar against other currencies—which has made it cheaper for most visitors to come here—has played a considerable role in the growth of inbound tourism to Australia. Table 3.2 shows what has happened to exchange rates. Over the period 1985 to 1994, costs within Australia became less than half for a Japanese traveller and almost as little for a German. It was also less for the others, except the Americans.

Table 3.2   Exchange rates, selected markets: the value of the Australian dollar on 30 June 1985, 1990 and 1994

Currency	1985	1990	1994
British pound	0.5136	0.4536	0.4721
NZ dollar	1.3850	1.3439	1.2258
US dollar	0.6655	0.7890	0.7291
German mark	2.0308	1.3180	1.1591
Japanese yen	165.6800	120.4100	72.2000
Singapore dollar	1.4866	1.4515	1.1114

Source: *Reserve Bank of Australia Bulletin*, December 1992 and July 1994 issues

The perception of cost at a destination is of great importance.

> . . . the number of Japanese tourists—traditionally Hong Kong's biggest spending visitors, and worth more than $HK9 billion in tourism receipts last year—is dropping as they grip their yen tighter.
>
> Japanese visitors for the first five months this year fell by nearly 14 per cent from the same period last year.
>
> 'Hong Kong is becoming too expensive even for Japanese tourists,' said one source at the Japan Travel Bureau in Hong Kong.
>
> 'Japanese travellers are changing their interests from South-East Asian cities to South-East Asian beach resorts. They are cheaper.'[4]

As we shall see, there is plenty of competition within the East Asia and Pacific Region. The position of the Australian dollar against other countries' currencies will have an influence on Australia's performance as an international destination in the future, perhaps as considerable an influence as it has in the past. But which way?

> A strengthening Australian dollar could threaten the tourism industry's otherwise lucrative future, a Federal Government adviser warned yesterday.
>
> Mr Geoff Carmody, the director of Access Economics, the economic consultant to the Australian Tourism Industry Association and a Government tourism adviser, said a rising dollar could make it difficult to sustain the significant growth expected in tourism in the next two years.
>
> 'Increasing world economic growth and the lagged effects of the lower Australian dollar in 1993 should combine to increase inbound tourism spending . . . Any lift in the dollar in 1994 will divert domestic spending offshore,' Mr Carmody told tourism industry representatives at a seminar in Sydney yesterday.
>
> 'But any significant lift in the dollar during 1994 could undermine the net inbound tourism spending benefits of economic recovery, both in 1994 and even more so in 1995.'[5]

Australia's inbound tourism growth

Australia's arrivals record since it first received a million visitors in a single year has shown annual growth rates of between 6.5 per cent and 26.0 per cent, except for the year following the 1988 Bicentennial. Table 3.3 shows how this compares with what has happened in the world and in the East Asia and Pacific Region.

To put Australian inbound tourism into historical context, it can be noted that Australia achieved 100 000 arrivals for the first time in a year in 1962, 200 000 in 1968 and one million in 1984. The table starts the following year, when a three-year acceleration began to give Australia a higher growth rate for the period shown in the table than the world or regional averages. In the last four years, Australia has come back to the East Asia and Pacific Region field, but overall it is an impressive growth record.

Table 3.3 shows that the world growth rates slowed during the period 1985–93. The 1990–93 average annual rate of 3.6 per cent is very close to that predicted by the World Tourism Organization for 1990–95: 3.2 per cent. The WTO annual growth rate forecast for 1995–2000 is 4.4 per cent, so that world arrivals should reach a total of 661 million by 2000. The arrivals forecast for 2010 is 937 million, approaching double the 1993 figure.[6]

Table 3.3   Tourism growth, 1985–1993: arrivals

Year	World	% change	East Asia/Pacific	% change	Australia	% change
	'000		'000		'000	
1985	329 634		30 389		1 143	
1986	340 800	3.4	33 505	10.3	1 429	25.0
1987	366 743	7.6	38 906	16.1	1 785	24.9
1988	402 123	9.7	45 092	15.9	2 249	26.0
1989	431 327	7.3	45 565	1.1	2 080	–7.5
1990	457 954	6.2	52 263	14.7	2 215	6.5
1991	456 502	–0.3	53 924	3.2	2 370	7.0
1992	481 672	5.5	61 306	13.7	2 603	9.8
1993	500 142	3.8	68 525	11.8	2 996	15.1
1986–93 average		5.4		10.9		13.4
1990–93 average		3.8		10.9		9.6
1985–93 % growth	51.7		125.5		162.1	
1990–93 % growth	9.2		31.1		35.3	

Sources: WTO; ABS

The WTO expects the East Asia and Pacific Region to come back to an average annual growth rate of 6.8 per cent for the rest of the decade, but this would still maintain it as the fastest-growing region in the world. There is no reason to think that Australia will not maintain its position as one of the growth leaders in the region.

Australia's average annual growth rates of 13.4 per cent for 1986–93 and 9.6 per cent for 1990–93 compare well on the world scale. Table 3.4 shows the fortunes of the world's top 20 tourism destinations between 1985 and 1992. It is significant that, of the five countries with the highest growth rates, three were accounted for by the only representatives from the East Asia and Pacific Region—China, Hong Kong and Malaysia. (The rise of Hungary to fifth place and Turkey's high growth rate are also worthy of note.) Australia, with 2 603 300 international visitors in 1992, was a long way from qualifying in that list, but it ranked ninth in the East Asia and Pacific Region in both 1992 and 1993 (Table 3.5).

Table 3.4   The world's top 20 tourism destinations, 1992

Rank 1992	Country	Tourist arrivals 1992	1985	Rank 1985	Average annual growth rate 1985–92
		'000	'000		%
1	France	59 590	36 748	1	7.2
2	United States	44 647	25 417	3	8.4
3	Spain	39 638	27 477	2	5.4
4	Italy	26 113	25 047	4	0.6
5	Hungary	20 188	9 724	11	11.0
6	Austria	19 098	15 168	5	3.4
7	United Kingdom	18 535	14 449	6	3.6
8	Mexico	17 271	11 907	9	5.5
9	China	16 512	7 133	12	12.7
10	Germany	15 147	12 686	8	2.6
11	Canada	14 471	13 171	7	1.6
12	Switzerland	12 800	11 900	10	1.1
13	Greece	9 331	6 574	13	5.1
14	Portugal	8 921	4 989	14	8.7
15	Czechoslovakia*	8 000	4 869	15	7.4
16	Hong Kong	6 986	3 370	17	11.0
17	Turkey	6 549	2 230	20	16.6
18	Romania	6 280	4 772	16	4.0
19	Netherlands	6 049	3 329	18	8.9
20	Malaysia	6 016	2 933	19	10.8
WORLD TOTALS		481 672	329 634		5.6

*Former Republic of Czechoslovakia
Source: WTO

Table 3.5   Arrivals in the top 10 tourism destinations in the East Asia and Pacific Region, 1993

Rank	Country	Tourist arrivals	% change over 1992
		'000	
1	China	19452	17.8
2	Hong Kong	7898	13.2
3	Malaysia	6800	13.0
4	Singapore	5848	7.4
5	Thailand	5714	11.3
6	Macao	3888	22.3
7	Indonesia	3400	11.0
8	South Korea	3331	3.1
9	Australia	2996	15.1
10	Japan	2100	−0.1

Source: WTO

Where they come from
Japan

Japan is the biggest source of visitors within the East Asia and Pacific Region and for Australia. In 1992 there were 9 085 000 arrivals from Japan in the region, well clear of the next biggest source, Singapore, with 5 546 000.

It is interesting to place Japanese travel to Australia in historical perspective. Overseas travel from Japan was restricted until April 1964, and most of the Japanese who came to Australia in that year (3307) were business people. This was the year the first detailed survey of the Australian travel and tourism industry was commissioned by the Australian National Travel Association and carried out by American consultants from Harris, Kerr, Forster & Company and Stanton Robbins & Co., Inc. Their report was delivered in October 1965.

> The comprehensive report made by this Mission concluded that a substantial travel market will develop in Japan, and to a lesser degree in Hong Kong and the Philippines, and that Australia could share in these markets by following a number of recommendations contained in the report for development of appeals for visitors and facilitation of their visits. The report states that a strong promotion programme will be required and recommended that a suitably qualified ANTA representative should be stationed in Tokyo.[7]

Among the recommendations in the report (which became known as the HKF Report) was the proposal that an 'Australian Travel Authority' should be created and funded principally by the Commonwealth Government. And so the Australian Tourist Commission came into being in 1967, not quite as the HKF Report envisaged; but it was charged with marketing Australian tourism internationally and it took over ANTA's existing overseas offices. It quickly moved to open an office in Tokyo and much imaginative work was done in the early promotional years.

However, progress in persuading Japanese tourists to come to Australia at the then high exchange rate was slow and it was not until 1979 that the magic number of 40 000 arrivals was reached—'magic', because to the Japanese travel industry at that time 40 000 was the threshold for a destination to be regarded as significant. Australia had 41 636 Japanese visitors in 1979. Smiling wholesale tour operators circulating at ATC's celebratory party in Tokyo gave assurances that Australia's long-held expectations were about to be fulfilled.[8]

It took some time. Four years after that, in 1983, the number of Japanese visitors was 71 813: good, but not very good. But in 1989, ten years after that first milestone was reached, the number had really moved—to 349 500. The Japanese were changing Australia's outlook on tourism.

Other markets

It had been anticipated at the beginning of the 1980s that Taiwan and South Korea, with their standards of living rising from manufacturing success, would lift the restrictions on their citizens travelling overseas on holidays. This they did, and now they too are contributing strongly to Australia's inbound growth. Annual growth rates from North-East Asia, other than Japan, and South-East Asia, were exceptional in 1994, with the relatively new markets of Taiwan, Korea, Indonesia and Thailand leading (Tables 3.6 and 3.7).

Chart 1 on page 32 shows how arrivals from its own region are dominating Australia's inbound tourism: a very different picture from earlier eras. The proportion from the region is likely to grow even larger, as indicated by the growth in Chart 2.

Table 3.6   International arrivals in Australia, 1994

1	Japan	721 100
2	South-East Asia	487 800
3	New Zealand	480 400
4	North-East Asia	395 300
5	Other Europe	370 700
6	United Kingdom/Ireland	350 500
7	United States	289 700
8	Rest of world	266 200
TOTAL		3 361 700

Source: ABS Cat. No. 3401.0

Table 3.7   Growth rates from six Asian markets, 1994

Country	Visitors	% change 1994/93
North-East Asia		
Taiwan	142 500	31
Hong Kong	109 500	19
South Korea	110 800	78
South-East Asia		
Singapore	187 600	21
Indonesia	105 700	48
Thailand	66 800	44

Source: ABS Cat. No. 3401.0

Chart 1   Sources of Australia's international visitors, 1993

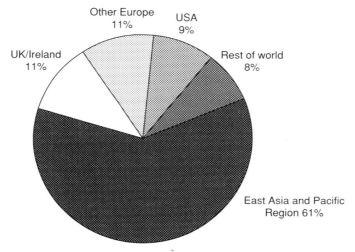

Other Europe 11%
USA 9%
UK/Ireland 11%
Rest of world 8%
East Asia and Pacific Region 61%

Chart 2   Australia's inbound tourism growth rate: percentage change, 1993–92

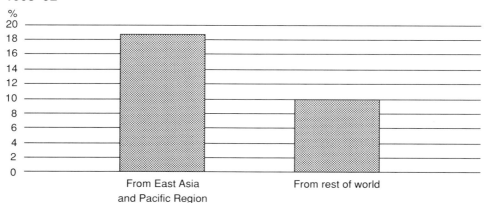

Inbound tourism in the region

Australians are considerable travellers in the East Asia and Pacific Region themselves, rating fifth in terms of arrivals in 1992.[9] Table 3.8 gives the 1992 arrivals in the region from both within and without (excluding Australia). By comparing the figures with those in Tables 3.6 and 3.7 it can be seen how Australia is tapping the main streams of tourists circulating in the region.

Table 3.8   Top markets for the East Asia and Pacific Region, 1992

Rank	Origin	Visitors	% of total arrivals in region	Average annual growth rate 1985–92
		'000		%
1	Japan	9 085	14.82	12.05
2	Singapore	5 546	9.05	10.24
3	Taiwan	4 253	6.94	26.40
4	United States	3 897	6.36	3.22
5	United Kingdom	1 977	3.22	4.73
6	Malaysia	1 891	3.08	5.45
7	South Korea	1 852	3.02	25.72
8	Hong Kong	1 750	2.85	9.88
9	Germany	1 260	2.06	13.11
10	Thailand	1 206	1.97	13.63
11	Philippines	817	1.33	11.77
12	France	793	1.29	11.04
13	New Zealand	769	1.25	7.92
14	China	610	1.00	18.67
15	India	553	0.90	−0.53
16	Italy	494	0.81	−1.05
17	Indonesia	485	0.79	6.55
SUB-TOTALS		37 238	60.74	10.52
REGION TOTALS		61 306	100.00	10.55

Source: WTO

Australia's share

We now have enough information to see how Australia performs in individual national markets and to calculate its share of the visitors from each of the top markets for the East Asia and Pacific Region. This is made clear in Table 3.9.

Table 3.9   The Australian market share of regional tourism, 1992

Origin	Arrivals in region	Arrivals in Australia	Australian market share
		'000	%
Japan	9 085	630	6.9
Singapore	5 546	117	2.1
Taiwan	4 253	64	1.5
United States	3 897	263	6.7
United Kingdom	1 977	290	14.7
Malaysia	1 891	60	3.2
South Korea	1 852	34	1.8
Hong Kong	1 750	75	4.3
Germany	1 260	90	7.1
Thailand	1 206	34	2.8
Philippines	817	16	2.0
France	793	25	3.2
New Zealand	769	448	58.3
China	610	19	3.1
India	553	10	1.8
Italy	494	27	5.5
Indonesia	485	46	9.5
TOTALS	37 238	2 248	6.0

Sources: WTO; ABS

Where Australians travel

ABOUT THIS CHAPTER

Australians have a different perception of distance from many other nations, because of the size of their own country and because of the European origins of a high proportion of the population. Those origins are a long way away, and this perception is reflected in Australian travelling habits. This chapter tracks travel by Australians.

Home and abroad

Australians have always been great travellers. They have a big land of their own, a whole continent. It has a superb coastline with thousands of kilometres of white sand beaches, a vast interior which is both dangerous and alluring, snow-capped mountains, jungles, vast flat plains, an assortment of pleasant offshore islands—the variety is endless. To all this, people have added a wealth of attractions and facilities for enjoying them, including world-class resorts.

Each year, a good part of the Australian population is on the move, vacationing at resorts, visiting another city for a sporting event or theatrical production, touring the outback, attending a business meeting or convention, skiing, holidaying with the family at the beach, or going home on leave, or for many other reasons.

The Bureau of Tourism Research (BTR), which is funded by the Commonwealth and State and Territory governments, measures the travels of Australians in their own country by 'trips'—a 'trip' being a journey of at least 40 kilometres away from home and including at least one night's stay away. Australians make about 50 million trips a year, mostly in their own cars.

The importance of domestic travel

Australians also travel in considerable numbers overseas each year—they made 2 267 200 overseas trips in 1993—but of course, Australians travel much more in Australia than elsewhere and much more within the country than overseas visitors. As we shall see in the next chapter, visitors contribute foreign exchange to the travel and tourism account which Australian travellers do not, but the importance of domestic tourism should not be obscured by the attention paid to international travel. Even now that visitors are coming here in their millions they contribute no more than the equivalent of about a third of the expenditure of Australians to travel and tourism in Australia.[10]

Australian travel overseas continued to rise through the early 1990s except in 1991, while 1992 was the down year for domestic travel (Table 4.2). Analysis of the 1993 domestic tourism figures showed a turnaround that began in the June quarter, when the number of trips increased by 16 per cent over the June quarter in 1992. Domestic travel then responded quickly to the economic recovery and cheaper travel—air travel continued to be cheaper than before deregulation and accommodation prices were still depressed. On the other hand, the number of trips overseas by Australians declined slightly in 1993.

Table 4.1   Where Australians travel

Within Australia 1992–93 by trips	'000
New South Wales	15 341
Queensland	10 604
Victoria	9 631
Western Australia	5 079
South Australia	3 774
Tasmania	1 752
Australian Capital Territory	1 103
Northern Territory	587
Overseas 1993 by visits	'000
New Zealand	350
United States	299
United Kingdom	240
Indonesia	201
Hong Kong	131
Singapore	97
Malaysia	83
Fiji	78
Thailand	71
Japan	45

Sources: BTR; ABS

Table 4.2   Travel by Australians, 1988–93

Year	Overseas departures	Domestic Trips	Nights
	'000	'000	'000
1988	1 698	46 177	216 313
1989	1 990	48 463	219 437
1990	2 170	48 957	218 253
1991	2 099	49 302	219 951
1992	2 276	46 081	207 510
1993	2 267	49 174	209 963

Sources: ABS; BTR

The effect of airline deregulation

The static figures of the recessionary years hide the effect of deregulation in 1990 on the Australian domestic airline business, which changed travel patterns markedly.

Major structural changes to the airline industry have occurred since then. Australian Airlines has been merged with Qantas, and the name Eastwest Airlines has disappeared. Two attempts to challenge Ansett Airlines and Australian Airlines were mounted under the name of Compass Airlines and everybody lost money. The biggest loser was Eastwest Airlines, which returned a deficit of $142.6 million in the 1991–92 year; far more than Ansett and Australian combined. In the aftermath of deregulation, Australia has one fewer major scheduled carrier.

But the airlines have more customers. Table 4.3 (page 38) shows what happened to the numbers travelling by air in Australia as a result of deregulation.[11]

The Bicentennial year of 1988 was a big year for air travel in Australia, but otherwise the 1980s was not a good decade for domestic growth. Then came deregulation in October 1990 and numbers jumped 27 per cent in the first full year, another 4 per cent the following year and a further 10 per cent in 1993. Australia was in recession in 1991, 1992 and the first half of 1993. The 1993 figures were nearly 80 per cent better than those for the last full year of regulation, 1989.[12]

Australians favour their own cars over all other forms of transport as their means of travel within Australia (for journeys that rate as 'trips'), but the plane is the most favoured form of public transport (Table 4.4). Most Australian car travel is intrastate, which makes the plane even more important for the longer journeys. Interstate travel accounted for 22.4 per cent of domestic trips in 1992–93.

Table 4.3 Domestic airline growth, 1982–93

Year	Passengers '000
1982	11 006
1983	10 241
1984	10 870
1985	11 802
1986	12 345
1987	13 074
1988	14 320
1989	11 149
1990	13 577
1991	17 304
1992	17 997
1993	19 921

Source: Department of Transport and Communications[11]

Table 4.4 Domestic travel modes, 1992–93

Passenger vehicle	%
Private vehicle	78
Plane	11
Bus/coach	5
Train	4
Rent-a-car, ship, boat, ferry	1

Source: BTR — <i>Domestic Tourism Monitor</i>

Table 4.5 Interstate travel in trips, 1992–93

Destination	'000
New South Wales	4 261
Queensland	2 219
Victoria	2 182
South Australia	894
Tasmania	337
Western Australia	332
Northern Territory	319
Australian Capital Territory	193
TOTAL	10 737

Source: BTR — <i>Domestic Tourism Monitor</i>

NOTES ON SECTION 2

[1] World Tourism Organization figures for the year 1993.
[2] The quote was from <i>Aerospace</i>, December 1993, p. 1. The detail about the Boeing 747 is from a Boeing Company news release dated 3 September 1994.
[3] WTO, <i>International Tourism in East Asia and the Pacific 1970–1993</i>.
[4] <i>The Australian Financial Review</i>, 17 August 1993, p. 41.
[5] <i>The Age</i>, 19 March 1994, p. 30.
[6] <i>Global Tourism Forecasts to the Year 2000 and Beyond</i>, World Tourism Organization, Madrid, September 1993.
[7] Harris, Kerr, Forster & Company and Stanton Robbins & Co., Inc., <i>Australia's Travel and Tourist Industry</i>, 1965, p. 110.
[8] The author was present.

9   Australia recorded 2 024 000 arrivals in the region in 1992, a year in which Australians took 2 276 300 trips abroad to all destinations. The regional figures include arrivals in several destinations by some people, so the numbers of arrivals are greater than the record of the number of journeys to the region.

10   Overseas expenditure is rising faster than domestic, of course.

11   These figures are aggregates of passengers carried by domestic services only to 30 June 1993. From 1 July 1993 they include all services over Australian flight stages operated by major Australian registered airlines. Over the period covered by the table, airlines have included the Ansett Group (including Ansett Australia, Ansett Express and Ansett WA), the Qantas Group (including Qantas, which commenced domestic services on 1 November 1992, Australian Airlines and Australian Airlink), Compass Airlines and Eastwest Airlines.

12   See Chapter 16 for a discussion on the effect of deregulation on business travel within Australia.

Evaluating different groups of tourists

Not all tourists are equal

TOPICS

- Volume versus value
- The world's top spenders
- What Australians spend
- Three forms of tourism in Australia
- Very special groups
- The Olympics and other big events

Spending on travel and tourism

ABOUT THIS CHAPTER

Things are not always what they seem. We talk as if the total number of arrivals from overseas were the barometer of our inbound tourism health, and perhaps this will always be the common perception. But tourists are people, which means they have individual and national characteristics. They stay for different periods while they are in Australia, do different things and spend widely differing amounts of money. We can group them, and put values on these groups, in a variety of ways. This approach makes a difference to how we evaluate what we gain from travel and tourism.

Australians and Austrians

Australians and Austrians are both big spenders on travel and tourism. Austria leads all the European countries on per capita expenditure, but even so the average Austrian spends less than three-quarters of what the average Australian does. As for Britons, on average they spend less than a quarter as much, while Germans spend about two-fifths and Greeks about one-fifteenth.[1]

Looking at national characteristics is only one way to assess the differences in tourists' spending habits. What travellers contribute to the various businesses servicing them, and ultimately to the national accounts, depends on how long they stay and what they do—why they were travelling in the first place.

Convention delegates have been called 'super-tourists'[2] because of what they spend per day, but in Australia backpackers spend more than any other type of international tourist. The reason is that they stay much longer: in 1992 they averaged 78 nights as against the overall average of 30 and spent on average $3267, as against the average for other visitors of $1760.[3]

Japanese spend more on shopping than other tourists (an average of $709 in 1993), but they stay the shortest time here. And so it goes. Tourism spending may not always be logical or symmetrical or predictable; there are a multitude of differences in the transactions which make up the Big Picture accounts. Because of this, relying on arrivals figures as the measurement of success in attracting overseas tourism can be misleading.

A record number of tourists visited Australia in January, and for the first time Asia provided the majority of the nation's visitors . . .

After adjusting for seasonal influences, 242,800 people visited Australia, an increase of 24 per cent on January last year, the Bureau of Statistics found. The previous highest number for any one month was 232,400 last November.

The rise follows two years of record growth for tourism in Australia despite the international economic slowdown. More than 2.6 million people visited Australia last year, an increase of more than 200,000 over 1991.[1]

Length of stay and expenditure

There is no question of the growth in the numbers of people coming to Australia, but arrival figures do not tell the whole story. The problem from a Big Picture viewpoint is that on average tourists have been staying a shorter time in Australia than they were a few years ago, and spending less. In the two years of 'record growth for tourism' mentioned in the report (1991 and 1992), visitor nights actually declined. Visitor nights, the measurement of length of stay, are a better measure of growth of tourism and changes in expenditure rates are important in reckoning the economic returns (Tables 5.1 and 5.2).

Table 5.1 Length of stay by overseas visitors in nights, 1990–93

Year	Nights
	'000
1990	66 019
1991	65 155
1992	61 820
1993	65 100

Source: BTR—*International Visitor Survey*

Table 5.2 Average visitor expenditure, 1990–93

Year	Expenditure
	$
1990	1 858
1991	1 819
1992	1 760
1993	1 794

Source: BTR—*International Visitor Survey*

Table 5.3   Average visitor length of stay in nights by country of origin, 1985–92*

Year	US	Japan	Other Asia	NZ	UK and Ireland	Total visitors
1985	25	10	29	21	38	28
1986	20	8	29	20	45	26
1988	25	9	31	21	48	28
1989	22	13	35	22	49	30
1990	25	13	38	22	57	32
1991	27	8	35	21	60	30
1992	25	9	32	17	47	26
1993	26	7	25	17	41	23

*The IVS was not conducted in 1987
Source: BTR — *International Visitor Survey*

Table 5.4   Source markets and expenditure contrasted, 1992–93

Ranking	Arrivals	%	Expenditure	%
1	Japan	23.4	Other Asia	27.1
2	Other Asia	20.9	Japan	17.0
3	New Zealand	17.2	Other Europe	15.0
4	UK/Ireland	11.0	UK/Ireland	12.6
5	Other Europe	10.4	North America	12.3
6	North America	11.5	New Zealand	10.9
7	Other	5.7	Other	5.1

Source: Australian Tourist Commission Annual Report, 1993

National characteristics have a role here. Japan has become the main source market, but Japanese people do not stay long in Australia: most of them get two short holidays a year. Just how short is indicated in Table 5.3.

How long people stay obviously affects how much they spend; we have seen that backpackers, the humblest of tourists in the eyes of many, actually outspend all others. The Japanese are quite easily outspent by other Asians, taken as a group (Tables 5.4 and 5.5).

Table 5.5   Per head expenditure by source market, 1993

Source	Length of stay	Spending per visit
	Nights	$
Japan	7	1 388
Other Asia	25	2 147
UK/Ireland	41	1 909
Other Europe	40	2 634
USA & Canada	28	2 008
New Zealand	17	1 118
Rest	28	1 807
ALL SOURCES AVERAGE	23	1 794

Source: BTR — *International Visitor Survey*

Weighing length of stay and expenditure

The differences in length of stay and expenditure have considerable importance for strategies of Commonwealth and State marketing organisations as well as enterprises concerned with getting the maximum benefit from overseas tourism to Australia. For example, while Victoria sees itself as disadvantaged in the Japanese market compared with New South Wales and Queensland, it is compensated to some extent in that its best overseas customers are the 'Other Asian' grouping, longer-staying and bigger-spending than the Japanese. In 1992, 28 per cent of overseas visitors to Australia spent at least some of their time in Victoria. Details are shown in Table 5.6.

The Enterprise View of this depends on the enterprise. Accommodation operators want people to stay longer, of course: their first measurement is in nights. On the other hand, a transfer bus operator wants numbers: the more people who come and go the better. The accommodation operator also wants people who pay rates that ultimately result in profits. Perceptions of value by different sectors of the travel and tourism industry can vary markedly.

> Australia still lagged behind other countries in return on room rates and, at today's levels, was at least 50 per cent underpriced in the world market, Mr [Darryl] Courtney-O'Connor, general managing director of Country Comfort told a Building Owners and Managers Association lunch in Brisbane.
>
> Mr Courtney-O'Connor said the position arose from the oversupply developed in the 1980s and the industry's headlong rush to attract the inbound market.
>
> It was a commonly held view that the inbound market was the 'holy grail' but it was important to understand it was the lowest yielding market source, he said.
>
> This could be altered significantly through attracting different inbound markets and changing the way wholesale operators were treated.[5]

Table 5.6 Market profile of overseas visitors to Victoria, 1992

Market	% of visitors	% of nights	% of expenditure
Other Asia	20	33	37
Japan	13	3	7
North America	18	14	15
Europe	16	16	14
UK/Ireland	13	19	13
New Zealand	15	7	7

Source: Tourism Victoria

The Big Picture view is that, while money follows the tourists, the amount of money per tourist is different and this is reflected in national receipts. It is reflected in world tourism rankings: the top four tourism countries remain the same in both international arrivals and receipts; but the United States, second to France in arrivals, jumps to the top of the receipts list, making more from international visitors than the next two countries combined. Australia makes an appearance on the international receipts list, taking sixteenth position (Table 5.7).

Table 5.7   The world's top destinations and earners, 1992

Rank	Country	Arrivals	Country	Receipts
		'000		$USm
1	France	59 590	United States	53 861
2	United States	44 647	France	25 000
3	Spain	39 638	Spain	22 181
4	Italy	26 113	Italy	21 577
5	Hungary	20 188	United Kingdom	13 683
6	Austria	19 098	Austria	13 250
7	United Kingdom	18 535	Germany	10 982
8	Mexico	17 271	Switzerland	7 650
9	China	16 512	Hong Kong	6 037
10	Germany	15 147	Mexico	5 997
11	Canada	14 741	Canada	5 697
12	Switzerland	12 800	Singapore	5 204
13	Greece	9 331	Netherlands	5 004
14	Portugal	8 921	Thailand	4 829
15	Czechoslovakia*	8 000	Belgium	4 053
16	Hong Kong	6 986	Australia	3 992
17	Turkey	6 549	China	3 948
18	Romania	6 280	Denmark	3 784
19	Netherlands	6 049	Portugal	3 721
20	Malaysia	6 016	Turkey	3 639
WORLD TOTALS		362 412		224 289

*Former Republic of Czechoslovakia
Source: WTO — *World Tourism 1970–1993*

CHAPTER	6

What Australians spend

ABOUT THIS CHAPTER

Australians are big spenders on travel and tourism, making the 'top twenty' list internationally. Nevertheless, it is at home in their own big country that they spend by far the most on travel and tourism. This chapter looks at what Australians spend on all forms of travel and tourism. Expenditure can vary considerably, depending on where you live.

Again we make the charts

Just as Australia has made the world's 'top twenty' chart as an earner from travel and tourism, so has it done as a spender on travel abroad, again occupying the same sixteenth spot on the ladder in 1992 (Table 6.1).

Table 6.2 on page 50 shows expenditure figures on international travel on a per head basis. The spending of Australians here is relatively low, no doubt because as a nation we spend so much on travel and tourism in our own country. On the other hand, a resident of a small European country (for instance), with nearby borders to cross, spends a higher proportion of his or her travel money internationally.

Spending within Australia

As we have noted, Australians spend most of their travel money at home, in their own country. Spending on travel and tourism within Australia goes in three directions:

- on trips away from home with overnight stays
- on day trips
- on the component of an overseas trip spent in Australia.

Table 6.1   The world's top spenders on international travel, 1992

Rank	Country	Tourism expenditure	Average annual growth rate 1985–92	Share of expenditure worldwide
		$USm	%	%
1	United States	39 872	7.19	14.48
2	Germany	37 309	16.50	13.55
3	Japan	26 837	27.82	9.75
4	United Kingdom	19 831	17.62	7.20
5	Italy	16 617	32.79	6.04
6	France	13 910	17.28	5.05
7	Canada	11 265	15.41	4.09
8	Netherlands	9 330	15.28	3.39
9	Taiwan	7 098	25.73	2.58
10	Austria	6 895	14.19	2.50
11	Sweden	6 794	19.37	2.47
12	Belgium	6 603	18.19	2.40
13	Switzerland	6 068	14.18	2.20
14	Spain	5 542	27.53	2.01
15	Norway	4 081	13.12	1.48
16	Australia	3 994	11.05	1.45
17	South Korea	3 794	29.96	1.38
18	Denmark	3 779	15.12	1.37
19	Finland	2 403	17.50	0.87
20	Singapore	2 340	21.09	0.85
WORLD TOTALS		275 297	15.28	100.00

Source: WTO — *World Tourism 1970–1993*

Australians make about 50 million overnight trips a year in Australia. Considering the scale of the country and the Australian view of distance, it is perhaps not surprising that in 1992 a Bureau of Tourism Research survey found that the average spent on each of those trips added up to $395. Multiplying that amount by the 46 081 000 trips taken that year shows that Australians spent $18.2 billion within Australia on overnight trips.

In addition, they spent $10.4 billion on day trips and more than $700 million on the domestic component of overseas trips. That adds up to $29.3 billion in travel within Australia in 1992. The Bureau of Tourism Research survey was of Australian residents 14 years old and over.

The survey broke down the main items of average spending on overnight trips. The result is shown in Table 6.3 (page 50).

Average day trip expenditure was $41. This was made up of $10 for vehicle expenses, $9 for meals, $8 for souvenirs, $3 for entry fees and $11 for other expenses.

Table 6.2 Per head expenditure on international tourism,[6] 1992

Country	Population	Tourism expenditure	Per head expenditure on international tourism
	millions	$USm	$US
United States	250	39 872	160
Germany	80	37 309	466
Japan	124	26 837	216
United Kingdom	55	19 831	361
Italy	58	16 617	287
France	57	13 910	244
Canada	27	11 265	417
Netherlands	15	9 330	622
Taiwan	21	7 098	338
Austria	8	6 895	862
Sweden	9	6 794	755
Belgium	10	6 603	660
Switzerland	7	6 068	867
Spain	40	5 542	139
Norway	4	4 081	1 020
Australia	18	3 994	222
South Korea	43	3 794	88
Denmark	5	3 779	756
Finland	5	2 403	481
Singapore	3	2 340	780

Sources: WTO — *World Tourism 1970–1993*; *The World Almanac and Book of Facts*

Table 6.3 Domestic travel expenditure: overnight trips, 1992

Item	Per trip	Per year
	$	$m
Accommodation	68	3 134
Meals	54	2 488
Petrol/oil	45	2 074
Plane fares	40	1 843
Shopping	32	1 475
Package tours	61	2 811
Others	95	4 378
TOTALS	395	18 203

Source: BTR — *Domestic Tourism Expenditure 1992*

Average expenditure within Australia on an overseas trip was $330, made up of $108 for duty-free items, $77 for clothes and shoes, $35 for non-duty-free souvenirs and gifts, $28 for accommodation, $17 for travelling to and from departure points and $65 for other expenses.

So what do Australians spend on travel and tourism overall—in and out of the country—in a year? Table 6.4, which puts international and domestic expenditure together, tells us. Australia's population at the end of 1992 was estimated at 17 572 000,[7] which gives a per head expenditure of $2235— that is, the average spending on travel and tourism for every Australian in 1992.[8]

Table 6.4   Australian spending on travel and tourism, 1992

Item	Aggregate
	Sm
International airlines	4 600
Other expenses abroad	5 349
Overseas trips: Australian Component	746
Domestic overnight trips	18 202
Day trips	10 420
TOTAL	39 317

Sources: ABS — Cat. No. 5302.0; Qantas Airways; BTR — *Domestic Tourism Expenditure 1992*[9]

The next table (Table 6.5) shows spending by residents of the States and Territories. Breaking this down to a per head basis, we find that in 1992 Australians spent an average of $1667 each on travel and tourism within Australia. The biggest spenders were people from the Northern Territory, the Australian Capital Territory and Western Australia. Northern Territorians spent twice as much on average as Victorians (Table 6.6).[10]

Table 6.5   Tourism spending by residents of States and Territories, 1992

State or Territory	NSW	Vic	Qld	SA	WA	Tas	NT	ACT
	$m	$m	$m	$m	$m	$m	$m	$m
Overnight	5 510	3 510	4 040	1 590	2 320	480	190	490
Day	3 611	2 413	1 974	570	1 176	271	268	137
Overseas component	320	144	97	46	100	10	9	20
TOTALS	9 441	6 067	6 111	2 206	3 596	761	467	647

Source: BTR — *Domestic Tourism Expenditure 1992*

Table 6.6 Tourism spending per head by State or Territory of residence, 1992

State or Territory	Population	Tourism spending	% of total	Per head
	'000	$m		$
NSW	5 979	9 441	32.2	1 579
Victoria	4 459	6 067	20.7	1 361
Queensland	3 072	6 111	20.9	1 989
SA	1 460	2 206	7.5	1 511
WA	1 667	3 596	12.3	2 157
Tasmania	471	761	2.6	1 616
NT	169	467	1.6	2 763
ACT	296	647	2.2	2 186
TOTALS	17 573	29 296	100.0	Av. 1 667

Sources: ABS — Cat. No. 3101.0, December Quarter, 1993; BTR — *Domestic Tourism Expenditure 1992*

Different forms of tourism

This chapter has shown how important travel by Australians, both out of Australia and, in particular, within, is to the national view of tourism and to the economy. Yet it is often forgotten.

> Tourism may just have had its best year, with the latest monthly figures indicating that the number of visitors in 1993 could have reached three million. More than 267,000 people visited Australia in October, according to the Bureau of Statistics. This was a 17 per cent rise on the number for October 1992.[11]

Here again is the popular press view that inbound tourism numbers are the whole thing: 'Tourism may just have had its best year'—that is, if 'tourism' means simply the number of overseas visitors arriving here.

There are three forms of tourism:

- domestic tourism, involving Australians travelling only within Australia
- inbound tourism, involving non-residents travelling within Australia
- outbound tourism, involving Australians travelling in other countries.

These three basic forms of tourism can be combined in various ways to produce the following categories of tourism:

- internal tourism, which comprises domestic tourism and inbound tourism
- national tourism, which comprises domestic tourism and outbound tourism
- international tourism, which consists of inbound tourism and outbound tourism.[12]

CHAPTER 7

Special categories of tourists

ABOUT THIS CHAPTER

People travelling for a particular purpose often make a bigger economic impact than others, and some events can be guaranteed to attract visitors from far and wide. These special cases are not only of interest to marketers and specialist travel organisers, but also to those who chart the economic impact of travel and tourism.

Why do people travel?

More people travel for holidays than anything else these days. The statisticians deal in broad categories and Table 7.1 (page 54) shows what they say about the purpose of travel for Australians and those people from overseas visiting Australia. There are no great surprises in the table, though it is interesting to note the higher proportion—and greater number—of Australians travelling overseas for business than overseas visitors coming here for business. The number of convention delegates, particularly international delegates, can vary widely from year to year.

Some broad statements can be made about spending on the basis of purpose of travel. People on holidays are interested in sightseeing and attractions as well as generally using the facilities and services available for visitors. Business visitors spend heavily on hotels and restaurants. Convention delegates are considered the best spenders of all on a daily basis.

Those who are visiting friends and relatives come from countries from which there has been migration. They stay longer than the other groups, they often stay privately and the people they have come to visit take them around; they do not have the same need as other visitors for accommodation, restaurants and other visitor services.

Now we will look at some particular things that draw travellers and can have a marked effect on travel numbers—and receipts.

Table 7.1 Purpose of travel for Australians and visitors to Australia, 1992

	Holidays		VFR*		Business		Convention		Other		Total
	'000	%	'000	%	'000	%	'000	%	'000	%	'000
Australians in Australia (trips)	18 207	40	13 492	29	6 430	14	960	2	6 992	15	46 081
Australians overseas (departures)	1 207	53	491	22	389	17	53	2	136	6	2 276
Overseas visitors (arrivals)	1 615	62	490	19	260	10	32	1	206	8	2 603

*VFR: Visit Friends and Relatives
Source: BTR — *Domestic Tourism Monitor*; ABS Cat. No. 3404.0

The meetings industry

As is shown in Table 7.1, a considerable number of Australians and overseas visitors travel to conventions each year. The meetings industry is involved not only in conventions, but also in seminars, business conferences and exhibitions. The Association of Australian Convention Bureaux includes incentive travel.[13] These components make up a lucrative business, with those visitors involved spending up to five times on average what other tourists do.[14] A range of specialists is involved in bidding, promoting and organising the various types of meetings.

World-wide, the value of the meetings industry has been put at $US80 billion and in Australia at $2 billion a year. It accounts for 15 per cent of all hotel room nights.[15] Almost half the international delegates are accompanied by one or more non-delegates, whose expenditure on sightseeing and shopping can be significant. The average length of a convention is about six nights, while the average length of stay by delegates is twelve nights. About a quarter of overseas delegates take official pre- or post- convention tours.

For the larger conventions, considerable investment in meeting places is necessary: Sydney's Darling Harbour convention complex and Melbourne's World Congress Centre are examples. Brisbane has the biggest of them all, a $170 million convention centre capable of seating 9000 in one area. At the other end of the scale is the Ayers Rock Resort Convention Centre, which can seat 300.

Rotary International's annual meeting in Melbourne provides an example of the impact of a single conference. More than 20 000 visitors from more than 100 countries came to the city for the meeting, held at the Flinders Park National Tennis Centre, and for associated events held over five days in May 1993. It was the biggest influx of visitors to Melbourne since the 1956 Olympic Games and generated an estimated $80 million for Victoria.[16]

Conventions on that scale are rare. Nevertheless, Adelaide hosted conventions worth $20 million to the State's economy in September 1993. They included the 6th World Conference of Operating Nurses (2100 delegates) and the 15th International Nutrition Congress (2500 delegates).

Obviously, organising a Rotary conference is a vast exercise—82 hotels were used to accommodate delegates; on one day alone there were 53 separate breakfast meetings at various function centres—but a great deal of preliminary work is involved in organising even much smaller meetings and the travel associated with them. The Association of Australian Convention Bureaux (AACB) surveyed 573 organisations and found lead times for the various markets as shown in Table 7.2.

Table 7.2   Lead times for meetings

International congresses	2–8 years
Association conventions	1–2 years
Companies	1–6 months
Exhibitions	1–2 years
Incentive travel	3 months–1 year

Source: AACB

Then the AACB combined a survey of three-to-five-star hotels and intelligence from its own national database to produce figures on the numbers of delegates in the various categories (see Table 7.3). Hotel income from meetings for that year was estimated at $541 million, which was calculated to be 17 to 30 per cent of delegate expenditure. Thus a total value of between $1.8 and $2.2 billion was arrived at.

Table 7.3   Meetings industry delegates: year to October 1993

Sector	Delegates	%	Room nights	%
Corporate	2 297 354	53	2 335 632	48
Association*	921 677	21	1 549 346	31
Government	596 963	14	618 820	13
Incentive	181 413	4	236 531	5
Other**	342 597	8	168 015	3
TOTALS	4 340 004	100	4 908 344	100

*Includes delegates not using accommodation
**Includes church and school groups
Source: AACB

Table 7.4 Delegates to Australian conventions: year to October 1993

	Conventions	Delegates	% of all visitors
International	201	80 240	2.9
National	515	244 500	0.4
TOTALS	716	324 740	0.5

Sources: AACB; BTR; ABS

Convention delegates represent only 7.5 per cent of the total, but they account for 25 per cent of room nights. Table 7.4 gives more statistics on conventions.

Incentive travel

Incentive travel is also a lucrative business, worth an estimated $US17 billion in the world in 1989, when 11.3 million people travelled on incentive trips. Industry experts estimate that incentive travel could be worth $US56 billion annually by the end of the century.

Reliable estimates of the incentives market in Australia are not available, 'but incentives and convention travel together are believed to account for 20 per cent of all tourism receipts in Australia'.[17] An Australian Tourist Commission trade show held in Sydney and Far North Queensland in 1992 is said to have generated bookings from incentive groups worth $43 million. From these groups, 14 500 delegates were expected to visit Australia, with each spending an average $3000.[18]

The Australian Tourist Commission reports considerable interest in Australia from incentive travel operators in the United Kingdom, Germany, Japan, the United States and New Zealand. Examples of large incentive travel movements to Australia are the April 1992 visit of 4500 saleswomen from the Japanese lingerie company Charle, followed by 2500 Amway sellers from Japan in early 1993. The Charle visit was worth $10 million to local suppliers.[19]

The domestic incentive travel business is well established in Australia, offering travel within Australia and overseas to Australian companies.

The events business

Events are big business for travel and tourism whether they are recurring, like the Formula One Grand Prix and the Ford Australian Tennis Open, or once in a lifetime for the venue, like the Olympic Games or an Expo.

Big theatrical productions also play an important part in attracting people to a city. In the early 1980s Cameron Mackintosh, the theatrical producer, approached a Sydney company connected with the Sydney Opera House and asked if it could sell a proportion of tickets for the upcoming production of *Cats* through the travel and tourism industry. It was given a target of 10 000 and sold 120 000 in the first year. The company, later called Showbiz Bookings, went on to hold an important position in the industry, selling tickets all around the world for Australian theatrical and sporting events at the rate of 350 000 a year.[20]

People flew to Melbourne from interstate and New Zealand at an average 1000 a week to see *Phantom of the Opera* when it played in that city from 8 December 1990 until 6 June 1993. Of 1.5 million ticket sales, 466 000 were to interstate visitors and 89 000 to overseas visitors, a total of 37 per cent. It was estimated visitor expenditure benefited Victoria by between $300 million and $400 million. In 1994, no less than 47 per cent of tickets to the Sydney production of *Phantom of the Opera* were sold by the travel and tourism industry through Showbiz Bookings.

Events at galleries and museums can also be big attractions. A single exhibition at the National Gallery of Victoria, the works of Vincent Van Gogh, shown between 19 November 1993 and 16 January 1994, attracted 20 000 overseas and 44 000 interstate visitors. Of the visitor total, 41 000 came to Melbourne for the exhibition. Visitor expenditure contributed $23.6 million to the State.[21]

More than 300 exhibitions were held in Australia in 1993, attracting 6.6 million visitors who spent $139 million on travel, accommodation and meals.[22]

International sporting events

Three major recurring sporting events which attract international as well as interstate attention are the Formula One Grand Prix—(held in Adelaide till 1995 but expected to move to Melbourne for the 1996 event), the Indycar Grand Prix on the Gold Coast and the Ford Australian Tennis Open in

Table 7.5   Three sporting events compared

Year of study	Event	City	Interstate visitors	Overseas visitors	Economic contribution[23]
					$m
1994	Indycar Grand Prix	Gold Coast	13 000	4 800	23.0
1990	Australian Open	Melbourne	16 500	6 900	16.5
1992	Formula One Grand Prix	Adelaide	16 100	2 700	31.6

Sources: *The Age*; Tennis Australia; South Australian Tourism Commission[24]

Melbourne. Only occasional studies of attendance have been carried out, so the figures in Table 7.5 do not refer to the same year. However, they do indicate scales of attendance.

World Expo 88

The six-month-long World Expo 88 in Brisbane in 1988 had a big impact on Queensland's travel and tourism industry and the State's economy generally. It attracted 15.7 million visitors, including 6.4 million interstate and 1.5 million overseas visitors. The analysis of this expenditure, on and off the Expo site, by all Expo 88 visitors is as follows.

Table 7.6 Expenditure by overnight visitors to World Expo 88

	Accommodation	Food and beverages	Transport	Shopping	Other	Total
	$m	$m	$m	$m	$m	$m
On-site		71.1		42.2	2.3	115.6
Off-site	364.8	492.8	313.5	401.4	224.9	1 797.4
TOTALS	364.8	563.9	313.5	443.6	227.2	1 913.0

Source: National Centre for Studies in Travel and Tourism for the Queensland Tourist and Travel Corporation — *Expo 88 Impact*

Direct expenditure The $1913 million of direct expenditure by visitors (Table 7.6) generated the following economic impacts in Queensland when both production and consumption induced flow-ons were considered:

- $4493.7 million of output
- $1280.5 million of income
- the equivalent of 58 929 jobs for a year.

Net impact This relates to the estimated $830 million of direct expenditure in Queensland during overnight Expo visits, which would not have been made if the event had not been staged. The economic benefit of this expenditure was estimated to be:

- $1954.1 million of output
- $558 million of income
- the equivalent of 25 778 jobs for a year.

Net additional This represents the economic benefits of total expenditure in Queensland during overnight trips, involving Expo visits, which would not have been made had there been no Expo, and which were additional to trips that would have otherwise been taken in Queensland during 1988.

Thus, those overnight Expo visitors who made special or additional trips to or within Queensland during 1988 for the purpose of visiting Expo generated an estimated total direct expenditure of $630 million. This is the initial output which, fed through the Queensland economy, resulted in:

- $1510.3 million of output
- $421.6 million of income
- the equivalent of 19 308 jobs for a year.[25]

The Olympic Games

The Olympic Games in Sydney are expected to have a much longer impact. Although the Games themselves will last only just over two weeks whereas Expo was on for six months, the impact of the Games has been assessed in years—14, in fact.

The Games were awarded to Sydney in 1993, but the impact was assessed in an economic impact study in stages from 1991, the first stage until 1994 being concerned with Olympic-related construction and other activity. The second period covers post-bid construction from 1994 to 2000, and the third period accounts for visits after the Games from people from overseas still reacting to publicity from the Games.[26] The expected sources of initial economic impacts were:

- the construction of Olympic facilities
- costs incurred in staging the Games (for instance, catering and security)
- expenditure by visitors from intrastate, interstate and overseas.

The study concluded that the Olympics would not only affect Sydney's economy, but its impact would also be felt throughout the Australian economy. Table 7.7 shows the assessment of the net impact in terms of the gross domestic product over a 14-year period.

The study also concluded that the Games would have a major impact on jobs (Table 7.8), again over the 14-year period, but commented that the distribution would be concentrated in the period from 1998 to 2000.

Table 7.7   The Olympic Games: net economic impact expected on GDP, 1991–2004

Region	Low case	Most likely	High case
	$m	$m	$m
Australia	6 352	7 336	8 230
New South Wales	4 093	4 587	4 790
Sydney	3 221	3 560	3 747

Source: KPMG Peat Marwick

Table 7.8   The Olympic Games: annual jobs expected, 1991–2004

Region	Low case	Most likely	High case
Australia	133 123	156 198	175 006
New South Wales	78 613	89 504	93 860
Sydney	64 846	73 089	77 551

Source: KPMG Peat Marwick

Governments would be substantial beneficiaries. The increase in economic activity would produce the additional revenues shown in Table 7.9 as a direct result of the Olympics.

The study concluded that the economic benefits of holding the Games would far outweigh any envisaged disadvantages and made these further observations. The Games:

- will have a small effect on the general price level
- will have a positive and significant effect on the balance of trade, adding more than $3.5 billion (most likely scenario) to Australia's net export earnings between 1994 and 2004
- are unlikely to affect the exchange rate
- are unlikely to create labour shortages, although it is conceivable that certain skill shortages may arise.

And what of the overseas visitors? What numbers are expected? The Australian Tourist Commission took this up after analysing previous studies, including the KPMG Peat Marwick Economic Impact Study.

The assessment of visitor arrivals resulting from an Olympic Games is perhaps one of the most challenging forecasting exercises in the tourism industry. All the difficulties associated with forecasting overall numbers to a destination are compounded by the need to identify the impact of a single future event as distinct from overall demand.

Analysing the impact of previous Olympic Games is of limited use, as differences in the tourism relationships and geographic distances between previous Olympic host cities and visitor origin markets make comparisons difficult.

Table 7.9   The Olympic Games: extra taxation revenue expected, 1991–2004

Government	Low	Most likely	Optimistic
	$m	$m	$m
Commonwealth	1 673	1 934	2 174
New South Wales	336	376	393
Local government	65	73	76

Source: KPMG Peat Marwick

The most complex component to estimate is the so-called 'induced' tourism impact, or the increase in visitors resulting from the additional publicity and awareness generated by the Olympics. This effect is spread over a longer time frame and is substantially greater in terms of numbers than the direct impact, which is Olympics event-specific and based on the number of athletes, spectators and officials visiting to attend the event itself.[27]

The ATC's forecast of the effect on overseas visits to Australia is markedly different from that of KPMG Peat Marwick, not only in the total effect, but also in the distribution over the 11-year period it studied. The two forecasts are compared in Table 7.10.

The difference in forecast expenditure can be gauged broadly by applying the average spending of overseas visitors in 1993: $1794 per visit. If the ATC's forecasts are right, then visitors would spend $500 million more in Australia in the Olympic year than expected by KPMG Peat Marwick in its most likely scenario. Over the period, the difference would be more than $1.6 billion.

While these numbers sound impressive, economists have put them into perspective. In examining KPMG Peat Marwick's figures, Geoff Carmody of Access Economics made these comments:

- The effect on inbound tourism, as forecast, was marginal: about 3.3 per cent of the ATC target for 2000 (this is before ATC revised its targets).
- The net effect on GDP [gross domestic product] is marginal: a net addition of about one-third of 1 per cent to GDP.
- The number of new jobs in the peak year is relatively small: 33 700.[28]

Table 7.10   Forecasts of extra visitors for the 2000 Olympics

Year	KPMG forecast	ATC forecast
1994	20 743	7 287
1995	44 820	11 071
1996	72 529	15 548
1997	104 089	34 557
1998	139 772	125 518
1999	149 765	207 439
2000	160 157	449 199
2001	171 013	482 589
2002	146 084	386 614
2003	116 990	241 004
2004	83 280	159 017
TOTALS	1 209 242	2 119 843

Source: ATC — *Targets 1994–2004*

His were not the only words of caution:

> The House of Representatives committee inquiring into the Olympics'
> implications for industry also heard the Sydney Games would lead to only
> a small increase in overseas tourists.
>
> In a submission to the inquiry, the Department of Industry, Technology
> and Regional Development says reports on the benefit to the economy
> overemphasised the impact of the Games . . .
>
> 'The actual effects are spread over many years, thus having a maximum
> impact of only one-third of 1 per cent of GDP to one-fifth of 1 per cent of
> GDP in 2000 . . .'[29]

But do such figures tell the whole story? The Games can leave a city with
splendid sporting facilities and, perhaps, much more. Barcelona, the
host city in 1992, used the Games as a catalyst for revitalisation. Among the
projects which were brought to fruition were a new airport, a ring
road, a telecommunications system, an improved sewer network, five new
beaches, expanded office and hotel space and a $2.4 billion waterfront
redevelopment.

> As Pasqual Maragall, Barcelona's rumpled, laconic mayor, admits, 'the
> Olympics is just a pretext. You've got to use it to produce change; other-
> wise it is a lost opportunity.'[30]

NOTES ON SECTION 3

[1] Australians spent about $2235 a head on travel in 1992 (see page 51). In 1993, Austrians were the biggest spenders on travel and tourism per head of population in Europe (*WTO News*, May/June 1994). The Austrian figure was $US1122 ($A1651 at the average rate of exchange in 1993— $A6795 = $US1). UK per capita travel and tourism expenditure was given as $US348 ($A512), for Germany it was $US602 ($A885) and for Greece $US100 ($A147).

[2] *The Age*, 17 March 1994, p. 19.

[3] *The Age*, 15 October 1993, p. 3.

[4] *The Age*, 20 April 1993, p. 1. 1991 and 1992 were not years of record growth. See Chapter 5.

[5] *The Australian Financial Review*, 3 August 1994, p. 33.

[6] Rounding off population figures in millions has created some anomalies, particularly with the smaller countries. Thus if Norway's full population had been used (est. 4 273 000 in 1991), the per capita expenditure would have been under $1000. Per capita figures should therefore be looked at for relativity rather than precision. Similarly with Australia's figures in US dollars, calculated in a period when the exchange rate fluctuated. Australia's population was just over 17.5 million at the end of 1992.

[7] It would be a little more; the figures for domestic expenditure do not include Australians under the age of 14.

[8] The international airline figure is a combination from the relevant ABS *Balance of Payments, Australia* quarterly, which gives 'Spending by Australians on Foreign Airlines' and an estimate of spending by Australians on Qantas air fares for the same period. Qantas does not release these figures but an estimate was obtained from published figures of Qantas accounts.

[9] ABS Catalogue No. 3101.0, *Australian Demographic Statistics*, December quarter, 1993.

[10] Again it should be noted that the figures for domestic expenditure do not include Australians under the age of 14. The population figures, as at 31 December 1992, include people of all ages.

[11] *The Age*, 13 January 1994, p. 5.

12 Adapted from *Recommendations on Tourism Statistics*, World Tourism Organization, Madrid, 1994.

13 Incentive travel is a form of bonus usually given for sales performance. The definition used by the Australian Tourist Commission in a 1993 brief was of 'the holiday travel incentive market, where people are given non-cash rewards for performance'. Big companies (e.g. motor companies) run incentive programs for dealers as a regular part of their marketing effort. Participants (e.g. major dealers) are often wealthy in their own right and the quality of the incentive is therefore high. There are many other kinds of incentive, including gifts based on performance. This is often referred to as the 'pots and pans' side of the business.

14 It depends on the conference. The Australian Tourist Commission's Delegate Expenditure Study, February 1990, found that the average total expenditure of international delegates, pre-paid and in Australia, was $3312 per delegate, compared with $1859 for all visitors. Average daily expenditure per delegate was put at $506.

15 These figures are taken from a fact sheet, *Facts and Figures on the Meetings Industry*, prepared by the research department of the Melbourne Convention Bureau, May 1994.

16 The estimate was made before the event for a State Government report. There was no post-event analysis.

17 *The Australian Financial Review*, 5 August 1993, p. 35.

18 *Australian Incentive Industry Market Overview*, Australian Tourist Commission, April 1994.

19 *The Australian Financial Review*, 5 August 1993, p. 5.

20 Interview with Michele Bribosia, Principal, ShowBiz Bookings, Sydney, May 1994.

21 Tourism Victoria supplied attendance and expenditure figures for *Phantom of the Opera* and the Van Gogh exhibition.

22 *Facts and Figures on the Meetings Industry*, Melbourne Convention Bureau, May 1994.

23 This means direct expenditure impact on the relevant State's economy. Included is expenditure by overseas and interstate visitors, competitors and visiting media. Included in the Formula One Grand Prix figure is an amount of $6.2 million for non-South Australian corporate facility holders. Different methodologies produce different results and we should be cautious in regard to the apparent relativity of economic contributions in this table. See Chapter 9 for discussion on methodologies for measuring economic impacts of events.

24 The Indycar Grand Prix study was carried out by consultants Ernst & Young, summarised in *The Age*, 16 May 1994, p. 1; the Ford Australian Open study was by the National Institute of Economic and Industry Research and the Formula One Grand Prix study was by Price Waterhouse.

25 *Expo 88 Impact*, The National Centre for Studies in Travel and Tourism for the Queensland Tourist and Travel Corporation, October 1989, p. 68.

26 The study on which this section is based was the Sydney Olympics 2000 Economic Impact Study, conducted by KPMG Peat Marwick in association with the Centre for South Australian Economic Studies. It is dated May 1993.

27 Australian Tourist Commission, *Tourism Market Potential—Targets*, 1994–2004.

28 'The Olympics, Asia and Tourism Yield', speech to Ninth Annual Australian Tourism Conference, Hobart, 15 October 1993.

29 *The Australian*, 2 September 1994, p. 3.

30 *The Age*, 22 August 1994, p. 11.

The economic impact

Tourism's worth to the nation

TOPICS

- Dispersing wealth
- Positive impacts
- Measuring impacts
- Effects on other industries
- Benefits to States and regions
- Balance of payments
- Taxation
- Regional tourism
- Employment
- Training

CHAPTER 8

The effect on the whole economy

ABOUT THIS CHAPTER

The wealth created by travel and tourism finds its way through the whole economy as those who receive money from visitors spend it in their turn. Travel and tourism impacts on other industries—not always favourably—but generally the nation enjoys a positive, considerable and growing economic benefit. The impacts are traced for inbound, outbound and domestic tourism.

Keeping the cost down

In determining the economic worth of travel and tourism, visitor spending is only the starting point. The effect of it has to be considered across the whole economy. It creates wealth, but for the nation to get maximum benefit it is necessary to keep down the overall cost to the community.

Expansion of tourism affects other industries; it can draw resources away or increase their cost. For example, mining and agriculture are affected by variations in the exchange rate caused by inbound tourism growth.

> . . . suppose an expansion of tourism exports pushes up the demand for tourism-related skilled labour. In the presence of a constraint on labour supply, this will bid up wage rates, increasing the production costs of all industries in the economy. Industries facing international competition will be unable to pass on these cost increases without losing sales. If a balance of payments constraint is also in place, the expansion in tourism exports will put upward pressure on the real exchange rate to prevent the trade balance from moving towards surplus. This encourages imports at the

expense of the production of domestic import-competing industries. It also reduces the competitiveness on world markets of traditional exporting industries in mining and agriculture.[1]

On the other hand, an expansion of tourism exports (inbound tourism) reduces Australia's reliance on mining and agriculture, Australia's traditional commodity exporting industries, and that has its benefits.[2] Export diversification reduces the volatility of our export prices and receipts and thus helps to soften the severity of economic cycles. It can also improve terms of trade, which means higher national income.

Positive impacts

On balance, travel and tourism has a powerful and positive impact on the economy. For example:

- **Economic activity** The total expenditure derived from travel and tourism in Australia was more than $40 billion annually in the mid-1990s. Australians spent about $30 billion a year and overseas visitors accounted for more than $10 billion. The world in 1994: a gross output of $3.4 trillion, 10.1 per cent of direct and indirect GDP. This accounted for 10.9 per cent of all consumer spending and 6.9 per cent of government spending.
- **Exports** Inbound tourism is an export. As such, in 1993–94 it generated $10.7 billion, 11.8 per cent of Australia's total export earnings. Earnings were up 16.2 per cent on 1992. Growth in tourism exports benefits the nation by adding to national savings or by providing the money to raise living standards.
- **Employment** About half a million people are employed directly or indirectly in the travel and tourism industry in Australia. The Department of Tourism gives a figure of 466 700 in 1991–92, or 6.1 per cent of the workforce—about 1 in 16. The world in 1994: 204 million employed, 1 job in every 9. Importantly, in Australia the industry has provided increased employment opportunities during recession years when unemployment, especially among young people, has been at record levels.
- **Taxation** Total indirect taxes derived from the travel and tourism industry in Australia in 1991–92 were around $3.6 billion. The world in 1994: more than $655 billion, 11.7 per cent of total indirect taxes.
- **Investment** Tourist accommodation projects worth $1.43 billion were scheduled to be completed in Australia in the three years to June 1997.

The world in 1994: $693 billion, 10.7 per cent of all investment, in new facilities and equipment.[3]

- **Decentralisation**   Tourism has provided investment in many regional areas of Australia and jobs in a number of areas outside capital cities where otherwise there might have been little opportunity for employment growth. The Cairns region is the most notable example.

Domestic tourism started to grow in mid-1993 after nine years of stagnation with an annual growth of less than 1 per cent. It is forecast to achieve a healthier growth at an average rate of 1.9 per cent until 1999. Nevertheless, the major growth in Australian tourism is expected to come from inbound tourism, with an average annual growth for the rest of the century of around 10 per cent.[4]

Inbound tourism expenditure

The Australian economy derives direct benefit from inbound tourism in these ways:

- Overseas tourists pay for international air fares on Qantas and Ansett Airlines.
- They buy goods and services in Australia.
- Foreign airlines spend money in Australia for landing charges, fuel, maintenance, food, sales offices, promotion and so on.

When Australian companies receive this money they may retain some as savings, but will use most of it to meet the expenses of doing business and paying their suppliers for goods and services. These suppliers then do the same kinds of things with their share, using it to pay their business expenses, including wages and dividends, and maybe to provide profits. And so it goes on *ad infinitum* until inbound tourism spending penetrates the far corners of the Australian economy. This is borne out in a study conducted in 1991 by Philip D. Adams and B. R. Parmenter[5] for the Bureau of Tourism Research. This study nominated 34 industries which produced goods and services for international tourism, but traced the effect of such spending on another 78 as well.

The importance of indirect spending

There are important consequences for companies involved indirectly in travel and tourism as overseas demand grows, taking up slack capacity and triggering a new round of investment.

Indirect spending includes investment in new plant and equipment: for example hotels, resorts, aircraft and motor vehicles. The money for construction and supply goes to companies which in turn pay it out for materials, wages, dividends, rent, insurance and so on and start the flow through the economy described earlier.

As overseas tourism increases, the firms supplying these goods and services raise their production levels to meet demand. This involves hiring more people, who then have money to spend. As the new plant and equipment is brought into use its owners have more income, too. The spending that results again causes successive rounds of demand affecting more and more industries, all the while inducing more production and more income.

Negative aspects

However, there are some other considerations.

- Not all plant and equipment is available in Australia. Some must be imported, thus affecting the balance of payments.
- It has also been found that:

Unless there is significant excess capacity in tourism-related industries, the primary effect of an economy-wide expansion in international tourism to Australia is to alter the industrial structure of the economy rather than to generate a large net increase in aggregate economic activity.[6]

How individual States are affected

We have already seen how a tourism expansion can 'crowd out' activity in the traditional export sectors, agriculture and mining, by causing a strengthening of the real exchange rate. This became a factor in the analysis by Adams and Parmenter (1993) of the effect on individual States of tourism growth in the period 1988–89 to 1994–95.[7] The analysis accounted for:

- the initial impact of overseas tourists' expenditure in each State and local multipliers
- activities within each State which supply the needs of the additional tourism directly and indirectly
- the implications of 'crowding out' of other industries.

Surprisingly, Victoria was projected to have most to gain from an economy-wide expansion of inbound tourism, followed by New South Wales, South Australia, Tasmania, Queensland and Western Australia.

Victoria has a relatively small share of international visitor nights (around 18 per cent), so its first-round stimulus is also relatively small. However, it has high scores in the aircraft and other tourism-oriented manufacturing industries, as well as having Australia's second most important air terminal. Furthermore, it is not as troubled as some other States by 'crowding out'; agriculture and mining are not so important to it as export industries.

The other surprise from the analysis was the low rating of Queensland.

> The key reason for this result . . . is that although it is relatively heavily dependent on tourism, Queensland benefits relatively little from expansion in the associated investment activities, especially in the transport sector. In addition, it is more heavily dependent than most other States on agriculture and mining. Hence, although Queensland receives a boost from the direct effects of additional tourism, the indirect effects of crowding out in the agricultural and mining sectors provide a significant offset.[8]

Domestic tourism expenditure

Domestic tourism expenditure comes from four sources:

1 intrastate tourism which includes at least one overnight stay
2 interstate tourism which includes at least one overnight stay
3 day-tripping or excursionist tourism
4 the Australian component of outbound tourism.

Items 1 and 2 are the forms of tourism covered by the Domestic Tourism Monitor: trips away from home which include at least one overnight stay away. This tourism does not have such an impact as international tourism. If it grows and goods have to be imported to develop or sustain it, it will influence the balance of payments, but not as much as inbound tourism, with its higher growth rate. Similarly, it is not likely to draw off resources or otherwise affect other industries to anything like the same extent.

How deregulation changed travel patterns

However, travel patterns changed as a result of deregulation of domestic airlines in late 1990, even though there was not much difference in the total number of trips taken over the next few years. The increase in air travel had effects—some temporary, others not—on the composition of the transport sector and on destinations. Overall, the change was very significant and it continues.

In the coach sector, express and long-distance touring were so affected that three companies, Greyhound, Pioneer and Bus Australia, were forced to combine as Australian Coachlines under one ownership. (The company is now Greyhound, Pioneer Australia Ltd.)[9] Touring by private car declined at the same time and this took its toll on the business of the large referral accommodation chain members.

Loads on the *Indian-Pacific* transcontinental train were as low as 20 per cent during the air fare war that followed deregulation and services were cut from three a week to two. The train had to be given a $12.5 million upgrade to make it more competitive.

Air travel favours 'stayput' holidays; that is, holidays in which the vacationer goes to a destination (as at a resort) and stays there, rather than touring from one destination to another. The Northern Territory, primarily a touring destination, reported a decline of 19 per cent in domestic tourism in the year ending June 1992.[10]

Transfer of wealth

Domestic tourism spending includes money that would not have been spent if the trip had not been taken (for example, on fuel and accommodation) and money which would have been spent anyway (for example, on food and entertainment). It has been calculated that the latter amounts to about a quarter of all domestic tourism spending.[11]

However, all money is spent in different places from those where the travellers live; it transfers wealth from one place to another. What this meant for each State and Territory from trips including at least one night's stay away from home in 1992 is shown in Table 8.1.

Table 8.1   Spending on trips with overnight stays, 1992

State	From intrastate tourism	From interstate visitors	Total
	$m	$m	$m
New South Wales	2 800	2 340	5 140
Victoria	1 150	1 640	2 790
Queensland	2 600	2 500	5 100
South Australia	530	590	1 120
Western Australia	1 460	630	2 090
Tasmania	210	450	660
Northern Territory	60	710	770
Australian Capital Territory	*	460	460
Not stated			72
TOTAL	8 810	9 320	18 202

*Under $5 million
Source: BTR — *Domestic Tourism Expenditure 1992*

Day-tripping

Day-tripping is, by its nature, local. It includes:

- pleasure driving
- visiting friends and relatives
- visiting museums and art galleries
- going to theatres, operas, ballets, concerts and films
- visiting animal parks, wildlife reserves and zoos
- visiting entertainment or theme parks
- attending special events
- participating in sport
- going on business trips
- attending conferences or seminars.

It impacts initially on the suppliers of travel and tourism goods and services, including attractions, sporting organisations, petrol stations, food outlets and, in the case of conference delegates, hotels or other meeting centres. As in the earlier examples, this expenditure then makes its way through the economy by successive rounds of spending.

The overseas trip component

The same thing happens with the fourth category of domestic spending—the component spent in Australia on overseas trips. This benefit is weighted towards those States with major air terminals.

Total Australian expenditure

Putting all this expenditure together, the result for individual States and Territories is as shown in Table 8.2.

Table 8.2   Australian spending on travel and tourism in each State and Territory,[12] 1992

State or Territory	Intrastate	Interstate	Day trip	Overseas travellers	Total
	$m	$m	$m	$m	$m
NSW	2 800	2 340	3 611	320	9 071
Victoria	1 150	1 640	2 413	144	5 347
Queensland	2 600	2 500	1 974	97	7 171
SA	530	590	570	46	1 736
WA	1 460	630	1 176	100	3 366
Tasmania	210	450	271	10	941
NT	60	710	268	9	1 047
ACT	*	460	137	20	617
TOTALS	8 810	9 320	10 420	746	29 296

*Under $5 million
Source: BTR — *Domestic Tourism Expenditure 1992*

The balance of payments

The effect of outbound tourism

Australian outbound tourism impacts on Australia's balance of payments. Figures on outbound expenditure recorded in the current account—part of the balance of payments accounts—come from two sources:

- the spending by Australians on foreign travel
- the amount paid to foreign passenger transport companies. Over-whelmingly this means foreign airlines, but the Australian Bureau of Statistics also conducts a Survey of International Shipping Operations.[13]

The Industries Assistance Commission put this, together with additional information from Qantas, into a table in its 1989 report (Table 8.3, opposite). From this table, it is clear that Australia had a deficit on its travel and tourism account in that year. The next table (Table 8.4) shows a more recent year as a comparison; by 1992–93 the total of Australia's accounts associated with travel and tourism were in credit.

What is the balance of payments?

The impact of travel and tourism on Australia's balance of payments is of public interest, as evidenced by this newspaper headline: 'Deficit down $700m in tourist boom'. The report which followed began: 'The boom in foreign tourists and falling interest rates has cut Australia's current account deficit by almost $700 million in the first five months of 1993–94, easing fears that the current account will blow out as the economy recovers.'[14]

Travel and tourism has been a major item in Australia's balance of payments figures for many years, but it is only in recent times that this report could have been written. Inbound tourism and its effect on export earnings have been only of such significance since the late 1980s.

It was even later than that before exports exceeded imports in travel and tourism. Not until the year ending June 1992 did visitors spend more in Australia than Australians spent outside the country—a net gain of $290 million for Australia.

We all know the balance of payments is important, particularly in this era when we have been running up deficits, consistently buying more from foreigners than foreigners buy from us. Once a month figures are announced, the money market reacts and the balance of payments is presented by the media as a critical factor in our lives. To understand its importance and the role that travel and tourism plays, we need to understand the details.

Table 8.3   Direct expenditure flows associated with international tourism, 1987–88

Credits	$m	Debits	$m
Spending by foreign tourists in Australia	2 966	Spending by Australians abroad	3 610
Spending by foreign tourists on Australian airlines	1 511	Spending by Australians on foreign airlines	1 547
Other Qantas revenue (freight etc.)	622	Spending by foreign tourists in Australia on imports	500
Qantas earnings in Australia (import substitution earnings)	867	Qantas expenditure overseas	1 438
Foreign airline expenditure in Australia	716		
TOTALS	6 682		7 095

Source: Industries Assistance Commission[15]

Table 8.4   Direct expenditure flows associated with international tourism, 1992–93

Credits	$m	Debits	$m
Spending by foreign tourists in Australia	5 707	Spending by Australians abroad	5 599
Spending by foreign tourists on Qantas[16] and other revenue Qantas earned overseas	3 876	Spending by Australians on foreign airlines	2 499
Qantas earnings in Australia (import replacement)	1 397	Spending by foreign tourists in Australia on imports	970
Foreign airline expenditure in Australia	1 536	Qantas expenditure overseas	3 146
TOTALS	12 516		12 214

Source: ABS; Qantas[17]

The balance of payments is a tabulation of the credit and debit transactions between Australia and other countries and international institutions, drawn up and published like the income and expenditure accounts for companies.

Put another way, the balance of payments is a record of Australia's economic transactions with the rest of the world, many of which do not involve simultaneous payment (such as credit sales) and some of which involve no payment (such as goods provided under foreign aid programs).

All these transactions, which usually involve dealings between an Australian resident and a non-resident, are entered into a set of accounts which make up the balance of payments. The transactions are divided into two broad groups:

- the current account, which is made up of 'visible' transactions (that is, merchandise exports, reimports and imports) and 'invisible' transactions (tourism, banking, insurance and shipping, together with profits earned overseas and interest payments)
- the capital account, which includes Australia's transactions with the rest of the world in financial assets and liabilities. These include foreign borrowing and lending by Australian residents, equity investments and Australia's foreign exchange reserves.

In principle, the deficit (or surplus) on the current account should be matched by a surplus or deficit on the capital account. But in practice the difference is recorded in the accounts as a balancing item. The balancing item measures the net effect of errors and omissions.

The term 'balance of trade' is often misused; in fact, it refers only to the trade in merchandise (goods), one item in the current account.

The current account
The balance on current account is made up of the following:

- balance on merchandise trade: the difference between the value of goods exported to non-residents and those imported from non-residents (for example transport equipment, fuels, wheat, coal, computers, clothing)
- net services: the difference between the value of services provided by Australian residents to non-residents and by non-residents to residents (for example travel, freight, insurance and legal services)
- net income: the difference between the value of income receivable by residents from non-residents and that payable by residents to non-residents (for example dividends on equity investment and interest on borrowing/lending)
- net unrequited transfers: transactions in which something is given or received but nothing is received or given in return. For example, where goods are provided to a non-resident under an aid program or where an incoming migrant brings personal effects into the country, the offsetting entry is an unrequited transfer. The difference between transactions where no payment is received and those where no payment is made equals net unrequited transfers.

The capital account

The capital account provides information on Australia's financial trans-actions with the rest of the world, such as payments made and received for important exports and investments in shares, bonds, loans and so on. The flows covered by the account are grouped into two major categories:

- official capital: transactions involving State and Federal governments and the Reserve Bank
- non-official capital: transactions involving financial enterprises and households. (Government-owned trading enterprises, such as Telecom, are included in the non-official sector.)[18]

The role of inbound travel and tourism

Inbound tourism is an export trade because tourists from other countries bring money into Australia and that has the same result as if we sold goods overseas. Conversely, outbound tourism is an import trade. The focus these days is on our rapidly increasing inbound tourism, but this will not bring about an improvement in the balance of payments automatically.

> Whether or not inbound tourism growth generates balance of payments improvements depends critically on how governments manage macro-economic conditions. Unless conditions are such that increased inbound tourism expenditure is prevented from feeding into net additional demand for imports, increased tourism will not be reflected in an improvement in the balance of payments. If it is desirable that Australia's dependence on overseas savings fall in the medium term, then national savings must increase in order to finance any increase in investment induced by the increasing receipts from tourism exports. This would mean that Australia's dependence on overseas investment finance would be reduced. In the longer term, however, increased tourism receipts will add to higher living standards for Australians, which may be expressed, among other things, as higher import demand.[19]

The example of Qantas

Tables 8.3 and 8.4 (page 75) showed the importance of international carriers in regard to balance of payments. The next table (Table 8.5) shows relevant figures for Qantas in 1992–93.

Table 8.5 Qantas Airways assessed balance of payments, 1992–93

	$m	$m
CURRENT ACCOUNT		
Inflows		
Revenue earned overseas (passenger, cargo, mail, charter and contract work etc.)	3 055.4	
Sale of assets	697.7	3 753.1
Outflows		
Expenditure incurred overseas (fuel, materials, interest, landing fees, advertising, marketing, passenger costs and administration etc.)	2 052.8	
Income tax paid overseas	6.7	2 059.5
NET foreign currency current account inflows		1 693.6
CAPITAL ACCOUNT		
Inflows		
Aircraft lease reimbursements	123.0	123.0
Outflows		
Purchase of assets including aircraft financed under sale/lease-back arrangements and progress payments on future aircraft	661.1	
Aircraft loan and lease repayments	425.0	1 086.1
NET foreign currency capital account outflows		(963.1)
NET foreign currency balance of payments inflows		730.5
Import replacement		
Qantas airline revenue earned in Australia		1 397.0
TOTAL export contribution		2 127.5

Source: Qantas Airways

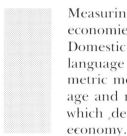

CHAPTER	9

Measuring the impacts

ABOUT THIS CHAPTER

Measuring the impact of travel and tourism on national or smaller economies, including its specific effects on employment, the Gross Domestic Product and other industries, is a complex task with a language of its own. In this chapter we discuss items like econometric models, input–output models, cost–benefit analysis, leakage and multipliers. We enter the world of equilibrium analysis, which deals with the interrelationships between sectors of the economy.

Many, many markets

Travel and tourism consists of many markets—for air, land and sea transport, for accommodation of many different kinds, for food and drink, for souvenirs and clothing, for amusement and attractions and so on. The interrelationships between markets are well established—or should be. If the demand for air transport rises, then that for accommodation can be expected to rise (but not inevitably; it depends on the length of stay being maintained); so will demand rise in other sectors, such as coach transfers. An increase in demand for accommodation will be accompanied by a rise in demand for food and drink, local touring, souvenirs and so on.

In the wider economy, the interrelationship continues. Aircraft and coaches will require more fuel and the demand for spare parts will rise. Demand for accommodation may reach the point where extensions—or new enterprises—are required. This will affect the market for building materials and land, as well as for many different kinds of labour.

The economy of Australia consists of thousands upon thousands of individual markets—for agricultural goods, for raw materials from the mines and forests, for manufactured goods, for land, for loans and so on. The outputs of some industries are inputs for others. It is an interlocking system in which anything happening in one market will affect many other markets. What co-ordinates the whole structure is the price system. Changes in surpluses or shortages are reflected in price changes. Price changes in one market are signals to decision-makers in other markets and they alter their behaviour in response.

Measuring tools

Inbound tourism to Australia is predicted to grow rapidly for the rest of the 1990s. This is discussed in Chapter 16, in which a number of forecasts for the level of overseas visitors in 2000 are compared. These forecasts were generated by **econometric models**. In the last chapter, the results of studies by Adams and Parmenter on the impact of inbound tourism growth on the Australian and State economies were discussed (see pages 69–71). Those results were also obtained through an econometric model.

Econometric models have been described as **input–output models** with elasticities, which are the measures of degree of responsiveness of one variable to another. However, before we discuss this any further, we should first look at two factors which affect economic impacts: **leakage** and **multipliers**.

Leakage

Not all the money from tourists may stay in the country or region where it is spent. 'Leakage' is the term used for the money that leaves a country or region. This may be paid for imports of food, fuel, equipment or other goods necessary for servicing tourists. It may be paid to international companies operating within a country's tourism industry, such as hotel management companies; it may be paid for reservations systems or outside training. It may be remitted as dividends or profits to investors from outside the country or area.

The proportion of leakage varies with the capacity of the local economy to provide goods and services that tourists want to buy; an economy with a diverse range of industries is obviously better placed than one which is heavily dependent on a few major industries and therefore must rely on imports for a variety of necessary products. It is also relevant to look at the type of tourist a country attracts. A poor country that attracts tourists who want to stay at five-star hotels, drink French champagne and eat Russian caviare is likely to have a substantial leakage problem.

Obviously, therefore, leakage varies widely throughout the world. In particular, it has been determined that some relatively poor island communities have not benefited nearly so much from tourism as might have been thought at first sight; most of the money that comes into the community has had to be spent outside again to buy the goods and services necessary to sustain its tourism industry.

> In the Bahamas, studies done several years ago indicated that as much as 79 per cent of the money coming into the region was needed to pay for necessary imports. This resulted in an important re-evaluation of the industry to determine its viability in relation to the high rates of 'leakage' for spending. In other countries, such as Greece or Yugoslavia, which are capable of supplying most of the tourists' needs domestically, leakage rates are much lower, 10 per cent and 2 per cent respectively; for these countries the economic benefits of tourism are far greater.[20]

Australia is in the low category. The Bureau of Industry Economics has estimated that, of each $100 spent by foreign tourists in Australia, only $17 is spent on imports. This was the figure used in the calculations of leakage in Tables 8.3 and 8.4 in Chapter 8 (page 75). However, this varies according to region and event. For example, a large proportion of the $8 million prize-money for the Ford Australian Tennis Open is won by players from overseas. Even with part of it remaining here in taxes and expenses, this would push leakage for the event above the average.

It will be noted later in this chapter that, in the preparation of tourism expenditure for econometric modelling, leakage is carefully calculated.

The multiplier effect

The multiplier is a measure of the effect on total national or local income of expenditure by tourists for transport, accommodation, food, souvenirs and whatever other goods and services they buy. It is the ratio of the change in national or local income to the change in the expenditure of bringing it about. This ratio is often used to indicate the importance of travel and tourism, sometimes in an exaggerated way. As we shall see, the use of multipliers is sometimes controversial.

We have already discussed how direct expenditure by tourists is only the beginning, the first round of spending. The money tourists spend is received by airlines, cruise ship companies, car rental firms, hotels, restaurants, souvenir shops and other operators. As the money is re-spent in successive rounds, the eventual increase in national income is greater than the initial spending. The overall effect of the income increase is called the multiplier effect. How great is it for travel and tourism in Australia? Here is an industry leader's opinion:

> Wackett says every dollar generated in tourism carries a multiplier effect of six times . . .[21]

A financial management guide produced by the Australian Bankers' Association discussed factors that influence dealings between tourism operators and bankers. It listed one of the factors as:

> ... the extent of 'multipliers' which operate, particularly in tourist areas. Several efforts have been made to identify the financial flow-on impact of tourism. Estimates range from approximately $4 to $6 of 'secondary expenditure' for every direct dollar of tourist expenditure. Especially in regions which have very strong tourism bases, firms such as the local butcher, accountant or builder all benefit from this flow-on effect, even though such firms are not defined as part of the 'tourism industry'.[22]

But there are differences of opinion about multipliers. Some economists are wary of reading too much into the multiplier effect at all, doubting that multiple counting of income is real in any sense; others question values unless they are produced over a short term, believing that variations in human behaviour with money preclude any formula being applied over, say, a year. However, there is less scepticism when a multiplier is calculated on something smaller than the national economy—for instance, when applied to a city or region.

It is essential, when measuring or applying multipliers in relation to a national or regional economy, that the input includes only money introduced into the country or region for travel and tourism; it is not money which residents would have spent one way or the other anyway. This may sound obvious, but there have been studies—of the economic impact of events, for instance—in which multipliers have been applied to the spending of residents; even multipliers derived from another economy have been used.

Input–output models

Input–output analysis has been the method most commonly used to quantify the impact of tourism. The structure of input–output models allows a prediction of the effects throughout the economy of changes in any one sector.

This structure is based on some simplifications. The basic unit is an industry that is assumed to use both labour and the products of other industries. It is assumed that sectors use their inputs in fixed proportions. Actual interrelationships are measured empirically and then used to predict the outcomes of various changes.

In Australia, input–output modelling usually starts with a matrix containing the 112 industries in the standard classification. The Australian Bureau of Statistics puts out an input–output matrix every two years or so. The input (or 'shock', for example a change in price of a commodity) brings about changes in the values in the matrix. This is manipulated mathematically depending on what kinds of results are required—economic impacts, multipliers, employment factors or whatever. Providing the input is usually simpler than it is for econometric modelling, because outside variables are not fed into the model, though they may be taken into consideration in preparing the input itself.

Econometric models

Econometrics is concerned with the application of mathematical and statistical techniques to economic problems. Econometric models are a theoretical system of mathematical relationships which try to capture the essential elements in a real-world situation.

We have already described econometric models as input–output models with elasticities. These additions—measures of degree of responsiveness of one variable to another—are hard to quantify, and therefore input–output models are often preferred. It is a simpler process. On the other hand, input–output models cannot provide a measurement of such important tourism matters as 'crowding out'.

The Adams and Parmenter studies (see pages 69–71) were conducted on a model called ORANI-F. This is the forecasting version of the ORANI multisectoral model of the Australian economy developed by the Institute of Applied Economics and Social Research at the University of Melbourne.

The Centre of Policy Studies at Monash University has a model unsurprisingly called MONASH, which is also a set of mathematical equations designed to capture the full range of interrelationships in the economy. MONASH is said to contain more detailed specifications in some areas.

MONASH was used by the Centre of Policy Studies and Syntec Economic Services to produce the fourth issue of *Guide to Growth: Australia's 112 Industries Ranked and Projected* with forecasts for the industries in the Australian Industry Standard Classification for the period 1992–1993 to 2000–2001. This was published by Syntec in December 1993. It was meant to cover every business activity in Australia but, of course, tourism is not regarded statistically as an industry and tourism activities are fragmented over a number of the industry categories. The study's comments on tourism were brief and of little value.

In their earlier studies, Adams and Parmenter used ORANI-F for specific tourism purposes, but from the opposite point of view. They projected the consequences of international tourism growth on the Australian economy, as measured by its effects on the 112 industries in the standard classification. They have noted that computable general equilibrium models, such as ORANI-F, are suitable for assessing the net benefits of tourism growth and do the job better than input–output models.

The first study was reported by Adams and Parmenter as *The Medium-term Significance of International Tourism for the Australian Economy* and published by the Bureau of Tourism Research in 1991. The following description of the input process is digested from that report.

ORANI-F is designed to project average annual growth rates of macro-economic and structural variables over the medium to long term. Outside the model, a detailed scenario (or economic environment) is compiled about likely developments throughout the forecast period.[23] The values of these variables are not determined within the model, but play a role in determining values of the variables within it. These outside variables typically include policy variables (such as the public sector borrowing requirement), variables governing conditions in the rest of the world (such as world interest rates) and variables associated with labour and capital markets (such as aggregate employment and the rate of technical change). In this case, they also included variables related to the size and composition of overseas visitor expenditure.

Obtaining projections of the effects of tourism growth on the economy from ORANI-F required detailed preparation of data for the shares of industry outputs consumed directly by international tourists and by parties involved with the transportation of those tourists. This was begun by compiling expenditure shares for a total of 28 visitor categories.

Next, specifying the tourism expenditure data in a form suitable for ORANI-F involved these steps:

1   The primary database for 1987–88 was compiled. This contained data on tourism expenditures by commodity expressed in current purchasers' prices. The principal source was the International Visitor Survey, with the addition of information from the Australian Bureau of Statistics and Qantas Airways.

2   The primary database was allocated to ORANI-F input–output industries.

3   The values of purchases of goods and services derived in Step 2 were converted from purchasers' prices to basic values to conform with the rest of the ORANI-F data. Basic values represented purchasers' prices net of indirect taxes (less subsidies) and of margins attributable to the wholesale, retail, transport and restaurant sectors.

4   Expenditures on imported items were removed from the aggregate expenditure flows in order to obtain flows from expenditure on domestically-produced items alone.

5   The expenditure flows derived in Step 4 were combined with data for total output by industry to form the estimated 1988–89 shares of domestic industry production purchased by overseas visitors, or by parties involved with the transportation of those visitors. The estimates showed that sales to international tourists generally constituted less than five per cent of the total sales of domestic industries—in fact, less than one per cent in many cases. The only exceptions were the shares in the production of air transport (31.3 per cent) and restaurants and hotels (13.3 per cent).

The ORANI-F model was then used to project the effect of additional over-seas tourism growth for the industries in the standard classification for 1988–89 to 1994–95. Projections were also made for the period 1994–95 to 2000–01.

Adams and Parmenter argue that input–output models exaggerate growth benefits because they assume that there are no supply-side con-straints and no price responses to increases in demand. They also ignore balance of payments and public sector effects. On the other hand, they write that ORANI-F:

> allows for supply side constraints, has an active price mechanism, requires specification of how balance of payments and public sector constraints are to be modelled, and allows for detailed inter-industry analysis. ORANI-F therefore is capable of picking up the various 'crowding out' phenomena needed to evaluate the net benefits—and intersectoral effects—of growth in tourism demand for Australia.

Cost–benefit analysis

Cost–benefit analysis is a methodology of a different kind. It is not used to measure impact on an economy, but is best suited for projects or events. In fact, it is not often used in Australian tourism. This form of analysis attempts to set out and evaluate the social costs and benefits of projects as well as the economic ones. For instance, in calculating the costs of a new airport, the losses in wellbeing resulting from noise, spoliation of areas of scenic beauty and so on would be included. A major problem with cost–benefit analysis is the difficulty of putting an evaluation on such matters. However, a Canadian assessment of methodology for evaluating the economic impacts of events (Getz, University of Waterloo[24]) concludes that cost–benefit evaluation is superior to the conventional means of assessing events through the use of multipliers or econometric models.

This method was used to evaluate Adelaide's first Grand Prix in 1986.[25] A group of researchers developed a methodology to ensure valid accounting of tangible costs and benefits as well as innovative measures of the intangibles. Tangible benefits were calculated using estimates of incremental income attributable to the event and the application of value-added multipliers, and were compared to tangible costs to yield a high and low benefit-to-cost ratio. Intangibles were compared separately, although the researchers developed several surrogate monetary measures for loss of time, accidents and amenity loss attributable to the race. Long-term benefits and costs were evaluated subjectively.

Getz does not recommend that 'such elaborate and expensive cost–benefit' methods be employed to measure the impact of events, but instead prefers a 'relatively simple approach' which can be summarised thus:

1 Measure return-on-investment, including direct job creation and numbers of tourists in attendance as well as the traditional profit–loss statements.
2 Establish through random surveys the relative importance of the event in motivating travel as well as increased length of stay and expenditure.
3 Calculate incremental visitor expenditure. (Gross visitor expenditure is not a valid measure of impact.) Reliable measures of average tourist expenditure must first be obtained, then an estimate made of the proportion of tourist expenditure judged to be incremental. Spending by residents should not be included. (Getz argues that there is no value in, and good reason to avoid, the application of multipliers or use of an econometric model to estimate total economic impact. Similarly, estimates of secondary employment impact are not helpful.)
4 Match claims of economic benefits to the host community with a statement of costs, including not only organisers' capital and operating costs, but also the grants and value of services invested in the event. Intangible costs and benefits, including imputed long-term effects, can be handled in a separate and subjectively evaluated statement. 'Attempts to develop surrogate monetary measures of intangibles are subject to many questions of validity and should be used very cautiously, if at all.'
5 Determine the distribution of costs and benefits. Specifically, it must be asked if the event is worthwhile if it is going to cause serious problems or costs for individual residents, even though it will generate a profit for organisers or overall economic benefits for the economy.

CHAPTER	**10**

Taxation

ABOUT THIS CHAPTER

We all expect to pay taxes, but industry bodies are constantly on the alert to protect travel and tourism from paying more than its share, inhibiting growth and costing jobs. A New York example shows what might happen if vigilance were relaxed. There is particular concern in some industry quarters about 'user-pays' charges.

The world's biggest taxpayer

Travel and tourism is a massive vehicle for governments and lesser public authorities to gather revenue. Given the scale of the economic activity involved it is no surprise that, according to the World Travel & Tourism Council, the industry is the world's biggest taxpayer, estimated to pay $US655 billion in corporate, personal and other taxes in 1994. In Australia, it has been estimated by the Bureau of Tourism Research that about $3.6 billion was derived in indirect taxes from the travel and tourism industry in 1991–92.

The tax collection comes in three categories:

1 the normal taxes—company, income taxes and so on—generated in business activity and everyday taxes paid by travellers (for example sales tax)
2 'user-pays' imposts such as air navigation charges, park entry fees and boat mooring charges; these are not taxes as such, but some believe the distinction is becoming blurred
3 taxes on tourists, such as bed or room taxes, which treat visitors as a convenient means of increasing general revenues. Travel and tourism is affected—because of the impact on its costs—by taxes levied on all road users, for instance. These include Federal fuel excise, vehicle registration, licence fees and State fuel taxes. In 1991 they amounted to $9.2 billion.[26]

As categories 2 and 3 are specific to travel and tourism, there is concern within the industry that it pays more than its share of indirect taxes, and this has a direct impact on its ability to create jobs.

'User-pays'

The Tourism Council Australia is particularly concerned about the growth of 'user-pays' charges. It identifies these areas:

- air navigation charges
- Federal Airport Corporation charges
- park entry fees
- vehicle registration fees
- fees for municipal facilities
- fees for maritime moorings, ramps and suchlike
- electricity costs which disadvantage island resorts compared with mainland facilities
- special water, sewerage, or other selective rates
- diesel fuel excise (applying to non-aviation and non-road transport operators).

Additionally, the adoption—with a vengeance—of the 'user-pays' concept by governments has now resulted in a whole range of government and quasi-government bodies identifying new charges for such things as:

- entry to national parks
- access to 'white water'
- access to publicly-controlled waterways
- contribution towards the costs of employee parking at airports.[27]

The Cairns Airport levy

The Cairns Port Authority, which owns and operates the Cairns Airport, has its own 'user-pays' revenue raising system; it levies a charge on airlines of $8 every time a passenger enters or leaves the airport. For years, Qantas absorbed the levy; however, in May 1993 it announced it was passing this on to its international passengers, itemising it on tickets as 'Australian tax—international passenger charges, Cairns'. Domestic airlines had always included the fee in their fares.

Taxing tourists

As for category 3, taxes on tourists to increase general revenue, Tommaso Zanzotto, the president of Travel Related Services International at American Express, as well as a World Travel & Tourism Council member, believes travel and tourism has become a soft target for this kind of taxation around the world. The WTTC review quotes him as saying: 'Taxes can be added almost unnoticed to hotel bills, airline tickets and car rentals, and there's nothing much the traveller can do about it.'[28]

Australia has not been in the forefront of this type of taxation, however, partly due to the vigorous opposition of the industry. The Tourism Council Australia, for instance, has resisted the imposition of a bed tax (a 5 per cent levy on paid accommodation in hotels, motels and so on) on the ground that it is inequitable, is a disincentive for investment and affects our international competitive position. Only the Northern Territory imposes a bed tax in Australia. It does not apply to backpackers or youth hostels. Nor does it fit cleanly into category 3, because all the money raised goes back into tourism — 75 per cent to the marketing budget of the Northern Territory Tourist Commission and 25 per cent to the Territory's regional tourist associations, where it has had a noticeable stabilising effect.

US hotel taxes

Taxes are prominent on American hotel bills. For instance, in Hawaii there are two taxes, a 'room tax' and a 'general excise tax', which together make up close to 10 per cent of the bill.

In New York there are more, lots more, giving the city what one general manager calls 'the dubious distinction of being the highest taxed city on this planet (as far as hotels are concerned)'.[29] First there is the 8.25 per cent state tax for rooms where the charges are under $100 a day. Over that figure an extra 5 per cent is added as a 'luxury tax'. Then there is a 6 per cent city tax and an extra $2 flat rate levied by the city, which goes up to $4 for a suite.

> I do not know the purpose for each and every tax. I know that the $2.00 City Tax is supposed to be allocated to our Visitors and Convention Bureau. Even though each hotel must pay the Visitors and Convention Bureau to be a member, the tax is meant to staff people in certain key locations for travelers aid and information. The other taxes are spread out, intended to pay police, fire departments and other government agencies protecting travelers and residents alike.
>
> The taxes act as a deterrent in attracting key conventions to our city. The hotels are reluctant to reduce room rates due to other imposed taxes,

such as, property taxes, revenue taxes, and generally high costs of operating hotels in the city. The city fire departments generate revenue through yearly inspections (costing the hotels $2000.00 per inspection; as many as 4 inspections during the course of a year). The buildings inspector also generates revenue every time he inspects the building.[30]

'Movement charge'

The Commonwealth Government has long applied a departure tax to people leaving Australia. From January 1995 it was raised from $25 to $27, called an 'international movement charge' and collected by airlines and port authorities instead of public servants.

> The departure tax has been a considerable irritant to travellers who were faced with finding the money to purchase a departure tax stamp prior to leaving the country . . .
>
> The collection by airlines or port authorities of an international passenger movement charge will be more convenient for travellers and lays to rest the cost recovery issue.[31]

But a tax is a tax, whatever way it is presented. The new charge was expected to raise an additional $5 million for the Commonwealth in 1994–95 and $43 million over four years.

Fringe benefits tax

The Tourism Council Australia is ever watchful for attempts to introduce new taxes which might inhibit the growth or profitability of tourism enterprises. When the Commonwealth Government proposed extending the fringe benefits tax to Australian business travellers in its 1993 budget, the TCA (then still called the Australian Tourism Industry Association) responded by inviting the Assistant Federal Treasurer to take part in a panel debate on taxation of the industry at the Australian Tourism Conference in Hobart. The conference heard arguments like this:

> Australia has learned, from bitter experience, that attempting to put a floor under wool prices just drives up supply that can't be sold. We should understand that putting a ceiling on prices will simply induce an increase in demand that will not be met. Both undermine Australia's income and

yield: both by corrupting market signals, either inducing excess demand or excess supply.

The proposed FBT on 'excess' domestic business travel is effectively a price cap on Australia's tourism export income. Business will not pay the excess, and tour wholesalers and domestic recreational travellers will quickly follow the business lead. Competition will force hospitality sector rates for meals and accommodation down, virtually across the board. Average inbound visitor spending will be capped as well. Export income from tourism will suffer. Jobs will be lost. The Budget deficit will be increased, not reduced.[32]

The proposal was later dropped.

The FBT continues to rankle, however. Airlines felt that a general increase in the tax in 1994 might cause some foreign airlines to cut back on staff based in Australia. The Board of Airline Representatives, which represents 32 airlines flying out of Australia, submitted to a House of Representatives Standing Committee inquiry into the impact of taxation on tourism that most overseas operators faced an effective FBT rate of 93.8 per cent, double the previous rate. The Board suggested that, where the FBT was applied to discount travel for airline staff, it should be levied at the cost to the employer rather than the much higher market value.[33]

The FBT has caused a severe reduction in the number of familiarisation trips available to travel agents. These have always been considered an essential educational activity.

CHAPTER	11

Regional tourism

ABOUT THIS CHAPTER

Regional tourism has been something of a vexed question over the years because of changes of attitudes under different State administrations and the lack of a national policy. Despite this, several regions have shown that local initiatives can influence inbound as well as domestic tourism. There is, of course, the example of Cairns.

Defining the term 'region'

Money can be brought into a region through agriculture or mining, through manufacturing or through tourism. There is now a realisation in Australia that tourism is often the swiftest, surest way. Recently Commonwealth funds have been allotted specifically to help regional authorities work out plans and improve facilities for tourists.

The term 'region' needs some discussion. It has been used already in this book in terms of the six regions into which the World Tourism Organization divides the world; Australia is part of the East Asia and Pacific Region. That is one concept, placing Australia in a global scene. Australia also has its own internal concept which treats regions as components of the country. There is such a tourism system, with regional tourism organisations.

The Domestic Tourism Monitor, which needs fixed borders, works on the system as it stood in the late 1970s. Since then some of the States have made adjustments to their regions, changing borders or, as in Victoria's case, changing the whole system.

In Australia, where States are dominated, in tourism as in other matters, by large State capital cities, regions are usually thought of as non-metropolitan areas (to some, 'lesser' places). In the future, Australia may adopt a more sophisticated regional system in which a particular geographical location and its associated tourism products are collected under a brand image, access is provided to major markets and marketing and plant development go hand in hand.

Swan Hill pioneers

An early example of how tourism transformed one country town and its region was provided by the establishment of the Pioneer Settlement at Swan Hill in 1966. (That was the year the Swan Hill Folk Museum was officially opened; the beginning of the project goes back to 1962.) It was still the only heritage park in Victoria when the Queen visited the settlement in 1970.

The Pioneer Settlement is an attraction built on the banks of the Murray, recreating a river town in which visitors can see how past generations lived and worked. It consists of a town with exhibits and working displays of vintage motor vehicles, early farm machinery, tractors and steam and oil engines. Horse-drawn vehicles ply the streets, craftspeople work in the trade shops and a paddle-steamer cruises the river. At night visitors are transported around the settlement for a 'sound and light' show.

The Pioneer Settlement transformed Swan Hill from a town that simply serviced surrounding agricultural enterprises into a tourism centre. Other attractions were developed, and now there are two historic homesteads, a military museum, several art galleries, wineries and pheasant and mohair farms. This concentration of product makes it worthwhile for people to stay longer than a day and has encouraged the growth of motel accommodation.

During the rural recession of the early 1970s, Swan Hill had the appearance of an oasis of prosperity, a prosperity which was due to tourism and which has lasted. The Pioneer Settlement remains the hallmark product, giving the region its tourism identity.

The Cairns concept

Cairns provides the best example we have of the larger regional idea, in which a whole section of Australia is provided with direct international access and the region marketed as a visitor concept. It always had the attraction — easy access to the Great Barrier Reef with its waters and its islands on the one hand, and rainforest country and the Atherton Tableland on the other. The 1980s saw it provide the access by creating an international airport. At the same time, a much greater range of tourist accommodation was built, a section of the city's centre converted to tourism shopping and other services added.

Above all, the catalyst for the growth in Cairns tourism was its airport, a local initiative. The Cairns Port Authority took over the airport under the Aerodrome Local Ownership Plan in 1981 and began turning it into an international airport capable of taking the biggest passenger jets. Stage 1 was completed in 1984 and Cairns tourism took off. For the rest of the 1980s, inbound tourism entry through Cairns averaged a 25.5 per cent increase per annum, contrasting with the national growth figure of 9.8 per cent.

The rapid growth continued in the 1990s: 240 362 people arrived or departed from the airport on international flights in the year ended June 1990, 327 905 in 1991 and 434 768 in 1992. By the 1990s, tourism was accounting for 30 per cent of economic activity in the Cairns region. Population had grown from less than 40 000 in the 1970s to nearly 100 000. In 1992, according to the Department of Employment, Education and Training, the Cairns region created more new jobs than any other Australian city, large or small.

Cairns authorities are predicting their airport will be the second biggest Australian gateway after Sydney by 2000.

> The director of marketing services with the Cairns Port Authority, Mrs. Gaye Scott, said that by 2000, Cairns expected that 23 per cent of visitors to Australia would be clearing customs through Cairns, compared with about 44 per cent for Sydney.[31]

The impact of tourism on the region's economy can be gauged from a comparison of production values in the 1950s and 1990s (see Table 11.1).

Table 11.1   Comparative value of production in Far North Queensland, 1957–58 and 1990–91

Industry	1957–58 Millions of pounds	% of total	1990–91 Millions of dollars	% of total
Sugar cane	18.966	47.2	168	8.5
Other agriculture	2.823	7.0	236	11.9
Total agricultural and pastoral	27.771	69.1	505	25.5
Fishing	Included above		106	5.4
Manufacturing	11.638	28.9	300	15.2
Mining	0.74	1.8	465	23.5
Tourism	Not recorded		600	30.4
TOTALS	40.149	99.8	1 976	100.0

Source: W. S. Cummings, Economic Research Services, for Far North Queensland Promotion Bureau — *Cairns and Far North Queensland: Tourism Statistical Profile*

Cairns was once a remote region in a continent far from the major world markets. The growth of travel and tourism globally and, of course, developments in transport gave Cairns its opportunity. Perhaps its very remoteness, which promoted self-reliance, was also important.

> As a frontier pioneering area for farming, grazing, mining and fishing, bedevilled by scarcity of labour, the region had developed a high degree of inventiveness, engineering and technical ability. During the 1960's, this inventive streak and engineering skills started focusing on the tourist industry, and produced the world's first underwater observatory at Green Island—a facility still in operation today. Most people are not good sailors, and during the 1970's and 1980's the region started coming to grips with problems of weather susceptibility in carrying tourists to the reef. The consequence has been that the Cairns tourist industry, with the support of its shipbuilding yards, has led the world in adopting advanced naval designs and techniques to produce high speed, ultra stable catamaran and wave piercer passenger vessels. In addition, semi submersible vessels have been developed for reef viewing.
>
> Air-conditioning for accommodation and coaches is now commonplace. 4-wheel drive coaches were developed to carry visitors into wilderness areas. In the course of servicing the region's tourism, industries such as shipbuilding, leisure wear, fishing tackle, tropical architectural design and landscaping, have developed capabilities and products that are gaining international markets on their own merits.
>
> Finally, as volume builds up, *success breeds success*. It has now become economical for the region to provide previously marginal aspects of tourism product. For the burgeoning youth market, new activities such as white water rafting, canoeing, and scuba diving have developed strongly in recent years. The Kuranda-based Aboriginal Dance Theatre has been so successful that it has recently completed a world tour. Shopping and night life availability has grown considerably, and a new standard and range of tourist accommodation has been developed with the erection of both 5-star hotels and youth hostels.[35]

More is to come, including a 2400-seat convention centre and the $200 million Cairns casino project. This will include a five-star hotel connected to the casino and a four-storey rainforest conservatory.

Broome charters

In 1992, the Broome airport runway was extended by 500 metres to take international aircraft. A series of charters from Singapore followed and occupancy rates at local resorts increased, as did property values. But the Shire

President said a development boom was unlikely, adding: 'We are not aiming to be another Cairns, but the flights will provide a boost to Broome and the Kimberley region.'[36]

Different communities have different ideas of what they want. It is important that there be some level of consensus because tourism does bring changes, some of them obviously good, while others impose costs. Apart from the irritation to some of having a lot more people around, housing is often an issue. Tourism can mean higher land values, which mean higher rates and a preference for higher-yielding property rather than low-cost accommodation. Where tourism dominates community life, it can cause disharmony.

> We do have concerns with social consequences. . . . the major issue that tourism has brought to this area has been a divergence of the community. There are locals who describe themselves as the people who have lived here for yonks, and do not want to see things change. There are the newer locals who have come into town and who now are permanent residents but who are going at 100 miles an hour to provide services to tourism . . .[37]

Addressing such concerns is now part of the process.

Commonwealth initiatives

It is now Commonwealth Government policy to foster regional tourism on the basis that it creates jobs, stimulates development and diversifies the regional economic base. The Government announced in its 1993 budget statement that it would provide $23 million over four years to improve the capacity and ability of regional Australia to attract international and domestic tourists. The program is providing grants to local governments, regional tourism associations and regional development organisations for:

- integrated regional planning
- diversification of the product base in regional areas to widen the drawing power for both domestic and international visitors
- provision of tourism infrastructure to increase the capacity of regions to support tourist attractions and to handle tourism growth in a sustainable way.

One of the problems with inbound tourism to Australia is that we have not been able to encourage adequate 'dispersal': that is, movement outside the capital cities and international gateways. Only a third of overseas visitors make overnight trips outside these centres.

One of the problems of regional tourism is that there has not been a national plan that incorporates them; though there has been piecemeal action on a State level.

CHAPTER	**12**

Employment

ABOUT THIS CHAPTER

Travel and tourism is not only a big employer; it is quickly becoming a much bigger one. It is also an uneven employer, largely because so many of the businesses are small. This chapter examines employment in a number of sectors, the growing professionalism apparent throughout the industry and the rapid increase in education both for people intending to enter the industry and for those already in it.

The prospects

By the early 1990s, travel and tourism was accounting for 6 per cent of the Australian workforce. Nearly half a million Australians were working in businesses directly or indirectly connected with travel and tourism. Despite the recession, the figure was increasing each year and by the end of the century was forecast to grow to between 600 000 and 700 000.

There is great variety in these jobs. Those working in the industry range from group general managers to dishwashers, from airline pilots to tour operators, from marketing executives to hotel porters—the list goes on and on. Those below were listed in a poster put out by the Department of Employment, Education and Training and Tourism Training Victoria; they are but a small fraction of the total:

airline passenger officer	kitchen hand
baker	luggage porter
bar attendant	pastry cook
car rental officer	receptionist
coach/bus driver	room attendant
cook	ship's purser
croupier	tour guide

flight attendant   travel consultant
hotel/motel manager   waiter

Airlines and big hotel companies offer the best examples of organisations with upward career structures. We will examine criticism that much employment in travel and tourism is low-paid and dead-end, but there is no doubt that as Australia's tourism expands and the workforce grows the opportunities for worthwhile careers also grow.

The number of management jobs among travel and tourism businesses is expected to increase by 21 per cent in the 1990s. This forecast was made as the result of a study on behalf of a group of organisations which included the Department of Employment, Education and Training, the Department of Tourism, the Department of Immigration, Local Government and Ethnic Affairs and the Australian Tourism Industry Association.[38]

The group, known as Tourism Workforce 2000, was given the task of analysing the travel and tourism industry's long-term labour needs. Its report, released in July 1992, forecast that the industry would create 16 per cent of total projected employment growth in Australia during the remainder of the 1990s.

Besides forecasting an increase of more than one-fifth in management positions over eight years, the report estimated that the number of service positions (for waiters, tour guides, flight attendants and so on) would increase by 51 per cent. Increases in full-time and part-time jobs, forecast by sector, were:

hospitality   108 000
transport   45 000
tourism services   39 000
tourism retailing   16 000[39]

![decorative rule]

The critics

In the late 1980s and early 1990s, travel and tourism was regarded politically as highly desirable in a period of structural change throughout the economy, job dislocation and high unemployment. But not everybody was enthusiastic. Here are three dissenting voices:

> Mr Colin Carter, a vice-president of the Boston Consulting Group, said that while huge hopes were held for tourism, it was essentially a low-wage, low value-added industry which could never make Australia rich.[40]

> Despite the variety of jobs generated by a tourist industry, the majority of employment opportunities are low-skilled, service jobs, often short term, and with limited career opportunities.[41]

Most hospitality occupations are semi-skilled or unskilled, with at most 20 per cent of the hospitality workforce employed in relatively skilled occupations such as chefs and managers.[42]

The implications in these statements about employment in the travel and tourism industry require further examination.

In 1989, while the Industries Assistance Commission characterised the hospitality industry as 'relatively poorly paid', it was not able to comment on travel and tourism employment as a whole because of the way statistics were compiled.

In 1993, the World Travel & Tourism Council took a more favourable view: it put the ratio of travel and tourism compensation as a whole to average compensation in Australia at 101.3 per cent. This is relative to an average for Organization for Economic Co-operation and Development (OECD) member countries of 104.6 per cent. The WTTC list for OECD members is printed in Table 12.1.

It is wise to treat generalisations about travel and tourism employment with caution, whether they are negative like the three quoted or, indeed, favourable like the figures in Table 12.1, simply because it is hard to get much that is useful from such generalisations—there is too much variety within the industry.

Most of the criticism comes from a study of labour market statistics. These are available for parts of the hospitality and transport sectors, but by no means cover the travel and tourism spectrum. There are business areas involved that do pay low wages and employ a high proportion of casual and part-time staff—this is borne out in the survey that follows—but there

Table 12.1   Ratio of travel and tourism compensation to average compensation

Country	%	Country	%
Australia	101.3	Japan	109.7
Austria	100.8	Luxembourg	110.7
Belgium	103.1	Netherlands	105.6
Canada	91.0	New Zealand	97.7
Denmark	101.8	Norway	103.4
Finland	102.0	Portugal	105.4
France	101.6	Spain	98.7
Germany	105.0	Sweden	100.9
Greece	105.1	Switzerland	108.8
Iceland	100.4	Turkey	92.7
Ireland	102.5	United Kingdom	108.1
Italy	107.2	United States	113.3

Source: *Travel & Tourism*, a Special Report from the World Travel & Tourism Council, October 1993

are others which pay well and offer good career paths or opportunities for people with enterprise to run their own businesses.

Similarly, it is difficult to accept the statement quoted that tourism is essentially a low value-added industry. Value-added is the difference between total revenue and the cost of bought-in raw materials, services and components. It is sometimes used to describe the contribution of an industry to the gross domestic product.

Value-added is spoken of broadly as 'wages and profits' but actually breaks down into four components: wages and salaries, indirect taxes, operating surplus or profits and depreciation. Everything else must be purchased from some other industry. Wages and salaries are the biggest component of travel and tourism value-added. Already we have seen that, according to OECD figures, wages and salaries in Australian travel and tourism are above the all-industries level (as they are for most countries).

Profitability in a year can vary immensely throughout the range of businesses involved, but some very good profits are made. Again it is difficult to generalise, but Table 12.2 suggests that travel and tourism's share of the total national value-added is not low.

Table 12.2   Share of travel and tourism and other selected industries in total value-added, 1990

Industry	Australia	Asia	US	Canada	Japan	Germany
	%	%	%	%	%	%
Travel and tourism	4 to 6	3 to 5	4	3 to 5	2 to 4	3 to 6
Agriculture	4	25	2	3	3	2
Mining	6	2	2	5	*	1
Food and beverage	3	3	2	3	2	4
Electronics	*	1	2	3	1	5
Motor vehicles	1	1	1	2	2	5
Textiles	*	4	1	1	1	2
Steel	1	1	1	1	3	3
Chemicals	2	3	4	3	5	7
Public utilities	3	2	3	4	3	3
Construction	7	5	5	8	7	6
Wholesale and retail trade	12	12	18	14	16	11
Communication	2	1	3	3	2	3
Finance and insurance	6	3	7	3	a	6
Real estate	14	4	21	20	17[b]	8
Health	5	1	6	3	10[c]	3
Education	5	1	1	1	d	1

* Less than 0.5.
[a] Included in real estate. [b] Includes finance and insurance. [c] Includes education. [d] Included in health
Source: Centre for International Economics — *Tourism: Australia's Passport to Growth*

The hospitality sector

More than half the jobs in travel and tourism are in the hospitality sector. This sector includes resorts, hotels, motels and other accommodation businesses as well as cafés, restaurants, public houses and licensed clubs. It employs a proportion of unskilled and semi-skilled people. This is obvious from the nature of the business; people are needed to wash dishes, carry bags and clean floors.

> The ACTU [Australian Council of Trade Unions] said existing hospitality career structures were very limited, with little opportunity for employees to move sideways to other occupations, or to advance within their own occupation. ATIA [Australian Tourism Industry Association] said unskilled workers were unlikely to have career prospects, and trained apprentices were unlikely to progress along a career path without further formal education. Since these occupations comprise more than 50 per cent of the hospitality sector labour force, this suggests limited career opportunities for many permanent employees.[43]

That statement, made in the Industries Assistance Commission (IAC) report of its inquiry into travel and tourism in 1989, is in line with the Commission's statement, already quoted, that 'most hospitality occupations are semi-skilled or unskilled, with at most 20 per cent of the hospitality workforce employed in relatively skilled occupations such as chefs and managers.'

The problem with the latter statement is that the IAC miscounted the figures it quoted from the 1986 Census of Population and Housing. These show that not 'at most 20 per cent' but 33.7 per cent of the restaurants, clubs and hotels workforce were in the 'relatively skilled occupations' of managers and tradespeople and there were others in classifications with career prospects.[44]

The hospitality industry may have some dead-end, poorly paid jobs; so do other industries. It depends on how you look at things. A case can be made for the hospitality industry offering better opportunities than is general in the workplace. Table 12.3 reproduces findings from the IAC report, on which some of its judgements were made. An additional column allows a contrast of the classification proportions with those in the workforce generally.

The biggest classification is that which includes waiters, waitresses and bartenders. These are job classifications in which it is possible to strive for excellence. The Catering Institute of Australia recognises grades of membership in management, marketing and craft streams. As an example of the latter, a person can qualify as a Master Craftsman 'after 6 years Supervisory experience at executive chef, head waiter, or chief steward level or a person accepted as an artist in their craft'.[45]

Table 12.3   Major occupations: restaurants, hotels and clubs, June 1986

Occupation	Males	Females	Total	% total industry 1986*	% total workforce 1994*
Managers and administrators (total)	22 301	12 805	35 106	16.5	11.2
Restaurant and catering managers/managing supervisors	5 549	3 953	9 502	(4.4)	
Accommodation and tavern managers/managing supervisors	11 211	7 010	18 221	(8.6)	
Professionals (total)	2 744	1 725	4 469	2.1	13.5
Para-professionals (total)	1 090	493	1 583	0.7	5.8
Tradespersons (total)	24 928	11 702	36 630	17.2	14.4
Meat trades	118	21	139	(0.1)	
Cooks/chefs	18 430	11 169	29 599	(13.9)	
Bakers/pastrycooks	295	114	409	(0.2)	
Clerks (total)	2 406	13 031	15 437	7.3	16.8
Accounting clerks	738	3 102	3 840	(1.8)	
General clerical	533	3 742	4 275	(2.0)	
Receptionists	565	5 102	5 667	(2.7)	
Salespersons and personal service workers (total)	24 141	48 723	72 864	34.3	16.2
Waiters/waitresses	6 497	23 495	29 992	(14.1)	
Bartenders	14 032	17 613	31 645	(14.9)	
Plant and machine operators (total)	893	205	1 098	0.5	7.1
Labourers and related workers (total)	15 849	26 358	42 207	19.8	15.0
Housekeepers	97	877	974	(0.5)	
Cleaners (including housemaids)	3 051	13 014	16 065	(7.6)	
Kitchen hands	5 851	10 558	16 409	(7.7)	
Inadequately described	930	759	1 689	0.8	
Not stated	737	861	1 599	0.8	
TOTALS	96 019	116 663	212 682	100.0	100.0

* Totals for each occupational group do not add up because only the major occupations within each are reported
Source: WTTC — *Travel & Tourism*; IAC Report No. 423; ABS[46]

The Restaurant and Catering Association of Victoria is considering ways in which a structuring of its membership can also recognise the achievement of standards of excellence. It caters for a section of the 'restaurants, hotels and clubs' classification in the ABS labour force classification—a section which employs more than 150 000 people in Australia,[47] about one-third of those employed in the travel and tourism industry.

There are restaurant chains which offer careers in management, marketing and finance, but generally the way ahead is characteristic of small business. Probably half the owners of restaurants and cafés are chefs.

The hotel scene

Three-to-five-star hotels offer a contrast within the same sector. Collectively, they employ more than 75 000 people but, of course, some of the enterprises are much larger than others and the job opportunities much more varied.

For those with management ambitions, attractive career paths are available in the bigger hotels and the chains—through the food and beverage or rooms divisions (or, less likely, marketing or finance) to a well-paid general manager's job or corporate executive status, perhaps with an international company.

At another level, in some of these hotels there are opportunities for 'artists of their craft', not only in the kitchens, but also in places of public contact: for example, doormen, head waiters and bartenders who have achieved a kind of celebrity status with their hotel's customers. Most of them would not change places with the general manager.

But, of course, not all accommodation establishments are in the three-to-five-star class. Small motels and caravan parks offer employment, but once again they are small businesses. There are 2850 three-to-five-star establishments in Australia,[48] about half of them three-star.

Table 12.4 shows that the five-star hotels, representing 2.8 per cent of the total number, account for 32.6 per cent of the workforce. The total of the major categories of visitor accommodation are shown in Table 12.5. The

Table 12.4 Employment in three-to-five-star hotels

	Total	5-star	4.5-star	4-star	3.5-star	3-star
Number of establishments	2 850	79	62	263	694	1 484
Number of bedrooms	131 629	22 036	6 878	19 556	26 285	43 434
Number of bedspaces	332 239	46 122	15 037	52 033	70 576	118 677
Number of employees	75 405	24 605	6 396	10 587	12 058	16 080
Average number of employees per establishment	26	311	103	40	17	11

Source: Building Owners and Managers Association (BOMA)

Table 12.5   Visitor accommodation, December quarter 1993

Type of accommodation	Establishments	Rooms or total no. of flats, units	Bedspaces
Hotels, motels, guest houses	4 832	166 743	478 366
Holiday flats, units and houses	1 493	35 486	154 103
Visitor hostels	414		24 960
Caravan parks	2 704		288 300

Source: ABS — *Monthly Summary of Statistics, Australia*, June 1994, Cat. No. 1304.0

three-to-five-star hotels are included in the 'hotels, motels, guest houses' of Table 12.5, so the remaining 1982 establishments account for only 35 114 rooms, or about 18 rooms per establishment on average.

Not all employees are ambitious

It is well to remember this about hospitality sector employment:

- Not everyone is looking for a career from it. A short-term or part-time job is often seen as desirable (for instance by students, young people wishing to travel and home-carers).
- Hospitality sometimes offers employment where there is little alternative (for example, outside metropolitan areas).
- Times change. The Australian Council of Trade Unions believes enterprise bargaining will result in a more permanent workforce in the less skilled areas of the hospitality industry.

> You couldn't work in the industry and support a family if you worked Monday-to-Friday day shift. In order to get a reasonable wage you've got to work the peak shifts . . . Now, by rearranging the award, you distribute the penalties throughout the whole workforce. That therefore creates flexibility for the employer but it also creates a living wage.[49]

The transport sector

Air travel now dominates intercontinental travel to the point where 99 per cent of people arriving in or departing from Australia do so by plane. Most travel within Australia is by private vehicle, but we have seen that the aeroplane can alter travel patterns and affect a whole range of businesses. The airline companies that bring about such change are big but, as in the other sectors, transport is also the province of small business.

Qantas Airways is the biggest company in Australian travel and tourism, employing 27 800 people, including 1500 overseas.[50] Ansett Airlines employs about 11 700; it also has staff overseas.

In May 1994, the Australian Bureau of Statistics reported that 34 300 people were employed in air transport within Australia[51]—not only with Qantas Airways and Ansett, but also with 48 regional airlines, which between them carry more than 2 million passengers a year—and in general aviation.

Far more people are employed in surface transport: 64 700 in road passenger transport, 51 300 in railways and 7800 in water transport.[52]

Australia owes much to its railways for early tourism initiatives—a number of the first State tourist organisations were originally branches of their sales systems. Tradition is carried on with the *Indian-Pacific*, the *Ghan* and the *Queenslander* trains, which cater specifically for tourists, and the marketing of inclusive tour packages on regular non-commuter services. The railways employ people with tourism backgrounds for marketing.

However, the government-owned rail systems carry most of their passengers within metropolitan areas; in 1992–93 out of 584 405 000 passenger rail journeys in Australia, 575 441 000, or 98.5 per cent, were in that category.[53] The railways are no longer dominant in the tourism business, though they have a role.

Water-borne tourism includes that available on the Bass Strait ferry the *Spirit of Tasmania*, paddle-steamers and other craft on the Murray River and cruise vessels on Sydney Harbour, the Hawkesbury River and around the Great Barrier Reef. Ocean cruising from Australian ports is increasing in popularity: 26 cruise liners docked in Australian ports in 1994.

However, it provides comparatively few jobs. The numbers given in this chapter for employment in water-borne transport include freight companies, which have nothing to do with tourism. In any case, the shipping companies involved are not big employers. TT Line, which operates the *Spirit of Tasmania*, has about 300 on its staff; two-thirds crew the ship and provide passenger services aboard, while 100 work ashore. Thirty people work in Cunard's Australian headquarters at North Sydney. Still, like so many companies in travel and tourism, the shipping firms have special appeal for some people.

Air and road transport are the main travel and tourism transport modes and it is significant that employment numbers for these have risen almost by half in the last decade, while those for rail and sea transport have declined (see Table 12.6).

Table 12.6   Transport employment changes, 1983–84 to 1993–94

Transport mode	1983–84	1993–94	% change
Road passenger	44 900	64 700	44
Rail	86 700	51 300	−41
Water	8 900	7 800	−12
Air	23 500	34 300	46

Sources: ABS — *1993 Directory of Transport Statistics*, Cat. No. 1132.0; *The Labour Force, Australia*, Cat. No. 6203.0

Table 12.7   Transport employment by sex, 1994

Mode	Males	Females	Persons
Air	21 000	13 300	34 300
Rail	47 800	3 500	51 300
Road	51 600	13 100	64 700
Water	6 500	1 300	7 800
TOTALS	126 900	31 200	158 100

Source: ABS — *The Labour Force, Australia*, Cat. No. 6203.0, May 1994

Unlike some other sectors of the travel and tourism industry, transportation employs far more men than women. Table 12.7 shows the numbers of males compared to females working in each category.

There are professional, technical and commercial careers in the air transport sector. Many people who have risen to senior executive positions have started in jobs classified by the statisticians as clerks or salespersons and personal service workers.

In Ansett Airlines, the usual way of entry on the commercial side is through reservations. This is where the sorting-out process begins: some people don't make it, some begin a work-life devoted to reservations, but most move on at various paces depending on their ambitions and the openings. Almost all promotion is from within and a big proportion of the staff are long-term employees.

Road transport

Coach companies provide express, touring, sightseeing and transfer services for tourism and are one of the major groups in the industry. The biggest express company is Greyhound, Pioneer Australia with 1000 employees, while McCafferty's Coachlines has 550. Of the big touring companies, Australian Pacific Tours has 380 personnel and AAT-King's 360, including overseas staff.[51]

There are coach companies everywhere, most serving local communities in country towns or suburban areas. They look after the touring needs of such diverse groups as schools, sporting clubs, senior citizens' clubs and special interest organisations such as art societies and garden clubs. Although some of these have expanded into substantial companies with, say, 40 or 50 coaches, most of the 2825 companies that belong to associations represented federally by the Australian Bus and Coach Association are small. The total number of employees is 20 000, which means the average number of employees per company is seven. The Association says multi-skilling is common, leading to greater efficiency.

Another form of high-profile road transport, rent-a-car companies, employ a total of about 1500 people.

Vehicles and fun

Apart from the main categories of transport that get travellers from here to there, with or without fun, there are a multitude of imaginative tour operations which involve special kinds of transport. A one-page classified advertising feature in a newspaper under the heading of 'Trains, Boats & Planes'[55] provides a sample:

Air safaris
Bareboat charters
Camp-sail safaris
Captain-a-cruiser
Castlemaine & Maldon Historic Railway
Explorer cruises
Flightseeing tours
Fly a warbird
Giant black marlin fishing
Gooney bird sightseeing flights
Karri Forest by Tramway
Lake cruises
Old Ghan train rides
Pichi Richi Railway (Quorn)
Puffing Billy tourist train (Dandenongs)
Rainforest river trains
Rent-a-yacht
Wilderness cruises
Yellow Water (Kakadu) cruises
Zig Zag Railway

There are not too many corporate ladders to climb here—indeed, some of the labour on the historic railways is voluntary—but the flavour of the list suggests why some people in travel and tourism enjoy their work.

The travel services sector
Travel retailers

Travel agencies in Australia employ about 14 000 people, mostly in small businesses, though American Express, Thomas Cook, Flight Centres and Ansett Airlines (through the Traveland group) own substantial numbers of agencies. Flight Centres owns 142 outlets (plus another 35 in New Zealand), American Express owns 119 and franchises around 100 others while Jetset owns 20, franchises 180 and has nearly 600 'associated agencies' with which it has commercial arrangements, though they do not carry the Jetset name. Traveland is another big player, with more than 100 agencies owned and about 160 franchised. Thomas Cook owns 52 large agencies.[56]

Most of the people in agencies work as 'travel consultants'; that is, they consult on travel to the public or corporate clients. This requires a knowledge of fares and ticketing procedures as well, of course, of destinations, attractions and facilities. The retail travel business is extensively computerised, though not as much as some principals would like.

Whether a consultant works for a big company, a franchised operation, an agency which is part of a co-operative or one that is fully independent, he or she (mostly likely she; about 80 per cent are women) works in a small business atmosphere.

There is a hierarchy among consultants in some agencies. A Melbourne agency which handles big corporate accounts insists on several years' experience before a consultant can be assigned to a major account. Staff members start with two years on domestic travel, then progress to working with a senior person on international travel. A high standard of performance is insisted upon (for instance, the agency does not automatically accept airline fare constructions) and a high rate of production is expected from each consultant.[57]

The agency business works on low margins and consultants are not highly paid. Some consultants earn much more, but the average wage in 1994 was about \$23 000–26 000. Career paths are usually horizontal rather than upward. An ambitious person in a big company agency can aim at a branch managership; otherwise, ambition means starting your own business.

There are travel incentives, though the fringe benefits tax has severely reduced the number of familiarisation tours available. Depending on the agency, there is access to sub-load (if seats are available) air tickets and travel incentives are offered by principals other than airlines.

> The way airlines offer sub-load tickets is often very discriminatory. The industry is largely made up of young, single women—you don't find many older, male consultants because they can't bring up a family on the pay—but the airlines usually offer two tickets to a married person but only one to a single person. If she does not want to travel alone she has to persuade a partner to pay an airfare. That means one is travelling sub-load and could be bumped and the other is travelling full fare with a firm booking. It doesn't work. The system is unfair: it values a married person's worth at twice that of a single person.[58]

For all that, there seems to be no shortage of aspirants for travel consultants' jobs. Also, the industry is changing. The number of independent agencies is declining; if they are not part of a fully-owned chain most agencies now are linked into franchises, co-operatives or some other grouping to exercise buying power in regard to travel products, to provide marketing programs and computer technology. There is a tendency towards larger operations, simply to create enough surplus from commission selling to meet overheads: the smaller suburban agencies may not survive except where they service a specialised niche market.

Wholesale tour operators

Wholesalers package tour products which are usually sold through the retail (travel agency) system. Sometimes they are companies which supply one of the principal elements in the package; in other words, they went into the wholesaling business to ensure people used their main product. Some examples are:

- the airlines; Ansett and Qantas are major domestic and international tour wholesalers, with a very big influence on where Australians travel on holiday
- coach companies such as Australian Pacific Tours[59]
- other operators who do not own tourism plant but simply buy services from those who do. An example: in 1841, an Englishman named Thomas Cook chartered a train to take a group to a Temperance Society meeting, but he did not become a railwayman. He extended his itineraries beyond a single train ride—around the world in fact; he guided his clients as far from home as Australia by whatever transport was necessary. His name lives on and so does his example.[60]

Tour operators in Australia do business in domestic, inbound and outbound tourism. Jetset, which we have seen is also in retail travel, is the biggest tour operator in the country and is in all three fields. Overall, it employs nearly 1000 people. A directory produced by one of the travel trade newspapers lists 329 outbound operators, 94 inbound operators and 225 domestic operators.[61] There is duplication, as some companies operate in more than one field.

Tour operations, particularly where international financial transactions are involved, is not an easy business. The life of a tour guide may appeal to some, but it is the behind-the-scenes work that counts and that involves a great amount of detail. Substantial tour operators today are therefore highly computerised. The bigger ones employ their own data processing experts and they need skilled financial controllers. Although many tour operations are started with the drive and imagination of entrepreneurs, as they grow and mature the operators find they need people who have trained minds.

They also need reservations people; about half of one operator's head office staff of 80 are in reservations. Overall, the work is varied. Developing the product, marketing it, selling it and seeing that it operates successfully is a chain of activity requiring different skills along the way.

That is not to say all tour operators are big companies; they are not. Some are small, with one or two people having a hand in most or all of the functions required.

There is no particular career structure across the sector. Companies vary according to size, the nature of their business and their history—whether their creators were entrepreneurs or whether they are part of or have connections with other, bigger companies.

Convention organisers and incentive travel houses

Often companies operate as both convention and incentive travel organisers, though there are examples of specialists in each. There are about 60 significant companies involved. They are not big employers.

The attractions sector

'Attractions' covers a wide range of enterprises, some of them run by governments. In some, employment is specialised; examples are art galleries, museums and zoos. Many are small businesses, but others are substantial enterprises; for instance, Movie World on the Gold Coast, Sovereign Hill at Ballarat and casinos. These employ large workforces, including a career executive group.[62]

The Australian Bureau of Statistics has put one section of the attractions sector under the microscope: amusement and theme parks.[63] The ABS defines an amusement park as a centre, often outdoors, that typically offers rides, games and shows for entertainment. A theme park is defined as similar to an amusement park but providing a range of entertainments and displays organised around a specific theme, such as the movies or pioneer life. A theme park may offer an educational as well as an entertainment component.

The theme park had its origins in the pleasure gardens of Europe, such as Ranelagh and Vauxhall of Georgian London. They have long gone, but Copenhagen's Tivoli Gardens celebrated its 150th anniversary in 1993 and continues to attract four or five million visitors each year. Walt Disney is said to have taken some of the ideas for his Disneyland theme parks from the Tivoli Gardens.

The Australian operations studied for the ABS report do not have that background, but did fit this criteria:

- They were primarily tourist attractions and operated on a commercial basis.
- Turnover was at least $150 000 in 1991–92.
- They were permanently based at a fixed site which included attractions operating at one site on a seasonal basis.

Operations excluded were:

- enterprises that primarily provided sporting facilities that focused on competitive sport
- recreational operations such as zoos and aquariums
- historic attractions and model displays
- entertainment complexes, including amusement arcades.

There were 72 parks fitting the criteria included in the 1991–92 census. Located mainly on the east coast, they employed 4614 people, had a gross income of $236.4 million and attracted more than 11 million visitors over the year.

Parks in Queensland attracted the most visitors (4.6 million) and earned the highest gross income ($140 million). Parks in other States were generally smaller in terms of visitors, gross income, employment and average spending per visitor. In fact, four parks dominated the scene, accounting for 60 per cent of gross income, 45 per cent of total employment and 32 per cent of visitors. About half the parks earned less than $500 000 gross revenue.

Table 12.8 gives a State by State summary. Queensland's parks provided almost half the employment, varying in the different quarters from 44 to 48 per cent. They also recorded the largest quarterly change in employment of all the States, an increase of 27 per cent to 2575 people between the September and December quarters. This occurred because of the large number of visitors to the Gold and Sunshine Coasts over the Christmas holiday period. How seasonality affected employment is shown in the next table (Table 12.9).

From this table we can see that not all people working at the parks were permanent employees; in fact, the proportion of casual and part-time employees was much higher than indicated by the seasonality figures—68

Table 12.8 Operations of amusement and theme parks, 1991–92

State	Businesses at end of June 1992	Total visitors	Employment at end of June 1992	Wages and salaries	Gross income
		'000		$'000	$'000
NSW	25	3 313	1 624	24 030	66 955
Victoria	18	1 948	588	7 631	19 215
Queensland	17	4 588	2 181	37 886	139 713
Others	12	1 182	221	2 905	10 554
Australia	72	11 031	4 614	72 452	236 437

Source: ABS — Cat. No. 8675.0

Table 12.9 Number of employees by quarter, 1991–92

State	September	December	March	June
NSW	1 757	1 973	1 585	1 561
Victoria	532	612	523	534
Queensland	2 029	2 575	2 112	2 076
Others	300	343	300	189
Australia	4 618	5 503	4 520	4 360

Source: ABS — Cat. No. 8675.0

per cent of total employment was classified as casual; that is, not entitled to paid holidays. Similarly, there was a high proportion of part-time employees (defined as working less than 35 hours a week): 41 per cent of the workforce in June 1992 (Table 12.10). Most permanent employees were male (59 per cent), while most casual and part-time employees were female (60 per cent and 58 per cent).

Another ABS study examined the way people were involved in cultural and leisure activities. A huge number of people are involved and most of them are unpaid. They may not always be recognised as part of the travel and tourism industry, but most of them are included because they aim to attract visitors (Table 12.11).

Table 12.10   Types of employment: end of June 1992

Type of employment	Permanent employees*	Casual employees	Total
Full-time:			
Males	868	481	1 349
Females	570	797	1 367
TOTAL	1 438	1 278	2 716
Part-time:			
Males	11	777	788
Females	40	1 070	1 110
TOTAL	51	1 847	1 898
Total:			
Males	879	1 258	2 137
Females	610	1 867	2 477
TOTAL	1 489	3 125	4 614
%	32	68	100

* Includes working proprietors of unincorporated businesses
Source: ABS — Cat. No. 8675.0

Table 12.11   Involvement in cultural and leisure activities

Type of activity	Paid only	Unpaid only	Paid and unpaid	Total
Museums	5 000	25 500	2 100	32 600
Art galleries	4 300	20 400	3 600	28 300
Libraries/archives	36 600	35 500	13 700	85 800
Heritage organisations	3 600	42 300	2 300	48 200
Art organisations	9 700	50 900	9 000	69 600
Art/craft show organising	7 900	113 200	12 900	134 000
Fete/festival organising	13 200	411 400	17 200	441 800
TOTAL INVOLVEMENTS	80 300	699 200	60 800	840 300

Source: ABS — *Work in Selected Culture/Leisure Activities*, March, 1993, Cat. No. 6281.0

The tourism retailing sector

Tourists like to shop, particularly overseas visitors. In fact, they spend about $1.5 billion a year in Australia on shopping.

> The Japanese take home armfuls of fluffy toy marsupials, the Europeans prefer Australian wine, but clothing has been revealed as the single most popular souvenir . . .[64]

The Bureau of Tourism Research surveyed shopping habits in the December quarter of 1992 and on that basis concluded that overseas visitors were spending more than $400 million a quarter then as against $250 million a quarter in early 1991. That is a rapid increase. The survey was taken in a year when we had some 2.6 million visitors.

Obviously, there is going to be a lot more shopping as numbers rise, providing a major export industry in itself. Some travel and tourism shopping is specific; for instance souvenirs and, in particular, duty-free shopping (which also services Australian international travellers). There are 164 duty-free outlets in Australia with sales totalling $700 million a year.[65] But travellers also buy from shops and stores that the resident population uses.

Travel and tourism should significantly increase the number of jobs in the retail sector during the 1990s—Tourism Workforce 2000 predicted 16 000 from 1992 to 2000—and the BTR shopping survey suggests they will cover a range of retailing establishments, not only in those specifically catering for tourism, and more in the big cities than in the purely tourism areas. Details from the survey indicate where expansion from tourism shopping might be:

- Sydney was rated by 31 per cent of overseas visitors as the best place to shop, Melbourne by 9 per cent and the Gold Coast by 7 per cent. Japanese visitors were most likely to purchase goods in duty-free shops, while Canadians were least likely.
- The Japanese liked souvenirs: 77 per cent of them bought fluffy Australian marsupials and other toys, followed by hand-crafted goods and jewellery. On the other hand, New Zealanders kept away from Australiana, hand-crafted goods and sheepskins, preferring to spend their money on clothing, duty-free spirits, perfumes, cosmetics and toiletries.
- European visitors rated wine as their most popular purchase, along with opals, gemstones and jewellery.

- Overall, clothing was the most popular single category (72 per cent), followed by fluffy toys (48 per cent), chocolates (35 per cent), books (32 per cent) and hand-crafted works, including paintings, carvings and sculptures (23 per cent).

Shopping has become big business for some tour operators. As an example, one Melbourne operator offers factory outlet tours in Melbourne and group shopping tours to Hong Kong. The company, Shopping Spree Tours, says it is the largest sub-contractor of coaches in Victoria and claims to have set a record with 53 tours in one day. Clients for the Melbourne tours are from all around Australia and New Zealand, and particularly from Adelaide and Sydney.[66]

The government sector

Government organisations are not always considered part of the travel and tourism 'industry'; it depends on the subject of the discussion. But governments are involved in travel and tourism and their departments and statutory authorities that carry out research, planning, co-ordinating, marketing and industry development functions obviously require a variety of professional skills. Table 12.12 shows the number of people employed in the frontline government tourism organisations.

Table 12.12   Employment in government tourism organisations

Government tourism organisation	Number of staff
Department of Tourism	136
Bureau of Tourism Research	15
Australian Tourist Commission	114
New South Wales	157
Victoria	109
South Australia	135
Queensland	360
Western Australia	160
Australian Capital Territory	47
Northern Territory	90
Tasmania	167
TOTAL	1 490[67]

Sources: Commonwealth Department of Tourism Annual Report 1992–1993; ATC Annual Report 1993; Tourism Commissions; Departments

Visitor, convention and promotion organisations

There are 11 visitor and convention bureaus in Australia. There is one in each of the capital cities except Darwin; in addition, there are the Gold Coast Tourism Bureau, the Far North Queensland Promotion Bureau, Tourism Albury/Wodonga and the Newcastle Visitor & Convention Bureau. They are all members of the Association of Australian Convention Bureaux and are membership organisations, usually with some money from State or local governments.

Outside the cities, there are a large number of visitor, informational and promotional bodies. These operate on two levels:

- A local tourist association primarily services visitors and develops products. It liaises closely with the community.
- A regional tourist association is a co-ordinating and marketing umbrella body responsible for promoting the region to target markets on behalf of and in co-operation with the local tourist associations and communities within the region.[68]

All these organisations are small—the Melbourne Tourist Authority employs 20 people in Melbourne and has two representatives overseas; the Sydney Visitors and Convention Bureau has a staff of 24 with three overseas representatives. A regional tourist association might have a staff of two.

Nevertheless, the various organisations discussed here have significance for those genuinely interested in a career in travel and tourism. In the visitor and convention bureaus there is often a great deal of skill directed at specific aspects of travel and tourism where the results are measurable, combined with a finely tuned knowledge of the area the bureau represents. The regional tourist bodies can be excellent training grounds for those who want generalist tourism experience (in contrast to understanding something of tourism from the point of view of an airline, motel or tour operator). Several of the Australian Tourist Commission's senior executives have come through the internal regional system.

The training boom

The rapid increase in inbound tourism has created a boom in another business: the education industry.

For those preparing to enter the industry, TAFE colleges offer courses in hospitality and tourism subjects. The latter are often aimed at those entering the travel agency sector, though there are general tourism courses at this level. This is also true of private providers, who offer a range of courses aimed at hospitality aspirants, those planning to become travel consultants or those who hope to achieve management status in some part of the industry. More than 20 universities have undergraduate courses in tourism management or hospitality and there is a growing number of post-graduate courses.

> In the old days with the hotel industry, everyone turned their noses up and said it was a job you did as a student, but it has been recognised as a profession now.[69]

Here are some examples that show current attitudes in the hospitality industry:

- The Southern Pacific Hotel Corporation, which has nearly 10 000 employees, usually recruits its potential senior managers from graduates and diplomates in hospitality and tourism and has links with universities for higher management development.
- Radisson Hotels draws on the training resources of its US-based franchisor, sponsors a hospitality course in its own name and is developing higher-level management education.
- ITT Sheraton is putting its 250 senior executives in Australia, Asia and the Pacific through Master of Business Administration (MBA) courses.
- Hilton International, which has a long history of training through its own Montreal centre and links with Cornell University, is also pursuing local education. In Melbourne, a private provider uses the hotel facilities for classes.
- The National Restaurant and Catering Association has a university-based tourism management course on offer Australia-wide, and the Victorian branch is working on a specific course for its own members.

Similar examples can be found elsewhere in travel and tourism:

- Australian Pacific Tours, which has operations in a number of countries, has been concerned with 'worldliness' as well as formal education. It has recruited a dozen graduates from the University of Heilbronn in Germany as well as graduates from Australian universities.
- An Ansett Airlines manager was once considered odd because he had a degree and extremely odd when he took time off to get a second degree. Now all his staff have degrees.[70] So do most people making their start in the commercial divisions of airlines.
- About half of Peregrine Tours' permanent staff of 20 have degrees. But none has qualifications specifically related to tourism. This is symptomatic throughout the industry—the general level of education of those

working in it is much higher than it was at the beginning of 1980s. But most of the degree-level education has not been specific to the needs of the job. It is one reason why there is a conviction that much more training—particularly management training with tourism content—is necessary for many of those already in the industry.

Universities have made a start with post-graduate courses, short courses and distance learning. More and more companies have opted for in-house courses made specific to their needs and some associations are offering courses produced for them by universities.

One of the problems is that, while a great many people are employed in travel and tourism and there are a large number of management positions, there is so much variation that it is difficult to find commonality in preparing course units. For example, the education needs of an independent restaurant manager and a hotel food and beverage manager are significantly different.

However, the travel agency business is more homogeneous and the Australian Federation of Travel Agents has set up the Australian Travel Agents Qualifications (ATAQ) program for agency staff members. It offers distance learning courses at five levels: Australian Travel Consultant (ATC), International Travel Consultant (ITC), Senior Travel Consultant (STC), Travel Supervisor (TS) and Travel Manager (TM).

The Tourism Council Australia has long been concerned with education and in 1980, with Qantas support, set up Tourism Training Australia, headquartered in Sydney and with branches in every State. It has achieved a great deal in bringing order into the various categories of tourism and hospitality education, in identifying core subject requirements, levels of standards and so on.

Foreign language requirements

The Tourism Workforce 2000 Report[71] put particular weight on the need for more Australians to learn the languages of our visitors. The report, issued in 1992, calculated that by 2000 Australian businesses would need to more than triple their number of tourism industry employees with high levels of language and cultural skills, especially for the Japanese and other Asian markets. That would mean about 100 000 multilingual staff employed in the industry by the end of the century.

While 62 000 Australians studied Japanese in 1990, the report considered 'only some of these will be able to provide the high level of skill required'. Apart from Japanese, the report identified a high demand for increased training and education in other Asian languages, including Korean, Cantonese, Mandarin and Indonesian. Greater skills were also required in several European languages, notably German, Spanish, Italian and French. Requirements for staff with these skills are spread across the industry and include accommodation, inbound operators, duty-free shops, airlines, attractions, tour operators and car rental operators.

The concern expressed in the report was reinforced in 1994, when another survey was undertaken to determine the industry's capacity to cope with non-English-speaking tourists. It was expected that, by the time of the Sydney Olympics in 2000, as many as 58 per cent of up to seven million tourists could come from non-English-speaking backgrounds as against 44 per cent in 1994. Expected changes in leading language requirements are demonstrated in Table 12.13.

Table 12.13   The top 10 language groups among overseas visitors

1991		2000	
Language of visitors	%	*Language of visitors*	%
Japanese	22.3	Japanese	22.9
German	4.2	Mandarin	8.4
Cantonese	2.95	Indonesian-Malay	7.2
Mandarin	2.2	Korean	5.2
French	1.9	German	4.6
Scandinavian languages	1.6	Cantonese	3.1
Indonesian	1.56	Thai	3.0
Italian	1.03	French	1.7
Korean	1.0	Scandinavian languages	1.1
Spanish	0.5	Italian	0.9

Source: *The Australian*[72]

NOTES ON SECTION 4

[1] Philip D. Adams & B. R. Parmenter, *The Medium-term Significance of International Tourism for the Australian Economy*, Centre of Policy Studies, Monash University, published by the Bureau of Tourism Research, Canberra, 1991, p. 14.

[2] In 1992–1993, rural products amounting to $17 079 million were exported. Mining exports totalled $29 269 million. Together they accounted for 77 per cent of merchandise exports. In the same year, services credits totalled $14 865 million, of which travel and tourism contributed $7848 million—ABS, *Balance of Payments Australia*, September quarter, 1993. Cat. No. 5302.0.

[3] Australian expenditure based on figures from the BTR's *Domestic Tourism Expenditure 1992* (see Chapter 6 and this chapter). Other Australian figures are from *Impact*, the Commonwealth Department of Tourism's monthly fact sheet, various issues. World figures are from *Travel & Tourism*, a special report from the World Travel and Tourism Council, October 1993.

[4] The domestic forecast is from *Forecast*, the first report of the Tourism Forecasting Council. There are a number of forecasts for inbound tourism, but all support a figure of an annual growth rate of about 10 per cent or more.

[5] Adams & Parmenter, *The Medium-term Significance of International Tourism for the Australian Economy*.

6   Adams & Parmenter, *The Medium-term Significance of International Tourism for the State Economies*, Bureau of Tourism Research, Canberra, 1993, p. viii.

7   ibid.

8   ibid.

9   Cheap air fares have also affected the only United States national bus carrier, Greyhound Lines Inc. In the first four months of 1994 the number of empty seats on Greyhound coaches rose to 53 per cent from 47 per cent a year earlier, causing a revenue loss and a reduction in share price. The main reason was loss of market share to discount airlines—*The Australian Financial Review*, 7 July 1994, p. 16.

10   This prompted a radical reshuffle of the Northern Territory Tourist Commission and promotional plans. The downward trend was reversed and by early 1994 Northern Territory tourism was reported to be vibrant again.

11   Bureau of Industry Economics, *Tourist Expenditure in Australia*, 1984.

12   There is no statistical collection of the Australian component of overseas trips within each State and Territory; the figures used in this table are the spending of Australian overseas travellers by State or Territory of origin. The great majority could be expected to spend their money within their own State or Territory, but this may not be true of the Territories or Tasmania. There are one or two other anomalies in the table—most of Canberra's day-trip expenditure is probably in New South Wales—but generally it gives a fair picture of the relative scale of Australian spending in the States and Territories.

13   In 1992–93 there were 5 192 300 arrivals by air and 15 500 by sea. Departures: 5 153 300 by air, 17 500 by sea.

14   *The Age*, 6 January 1994, p. 5.

15   Industries Assistance Commission, *Travel and Tourism*, Report No. 423, 29 September 1989, Appendix D, p. 3.

16   Qantas was still the only Australian international carrier in 1992–93. Ansett Airlines began international operations on 11 September 1993.

17   ABS *Balance of Payments, Australia*, September Quarter 1993, Cat. No. 5302.0. Foreign airline expenditure in Australia by ABS telephone service. Qantas financial analysis dated 6 September 1993. Spending by foreign tourists on imports calculated in the same way as the IAC report—using the Bureau of Industry Economics estimate of $17 in the $100 of spending.

18   The explanation of balance of payments has been drawn from 'An Insight into the Balance of Payments', contributed by the Balance of Payments Team in *What Figures*, Australian Bureau of Statistics, December 1993.

19   Adams & Parmenter, *The Medium-term Significance of International Tourism for the Australian Economy*, p. 7.

20   Sharon Dickman, *Tourism. An Introductory Text*, Edward Arnold (Australia) Pty Ltd, Melbourne, 1989, p. 153.

21   *Business Review Weekly*, 17 April 1992, p. 38, interview with Graham Wackett, Chief Executive, Southern Pacific Hotels Corporation.

22   Australian Bankers' Association, *The Business of Tourism*, Melbourne, 1993, p. 40.

23   Factors or assumptions affecting the outside-the-model scenario are called 'exogenous', those inside-the-model are called 'endogenous'. *Oxford English Dictionary* definitions: exogenous, 'growing or originating from the outside'; endogenous, 'growing or originating from within'.

24   Donald Getz, Department of Recreation and Leisure Studies, University of Waterloo, *Journal of Applied Research*, 16 (1): 61–77, 1991.

25   J. Burns, J. Hatch & T. Mules (eds), *The Adelaide Grand Prix; The Impact of a Special Event*, Centre of South Australian Economic Studies, Adelaide, 1986.

26   Australian Bus and Coach Association, *1994 Factsheet*.

27   *User Pays, ATIA Update*, undated. In a speech to the Australian Tourism Conference in Hobart, October 1993, the Chairman of ATIA, Sir Frank Moore, attacked what he called the 'virus' of user-pays. He said the principle was particularly harmful to national parks, which were being forced to impose entrance fees, turning people off without providing any real benefit to the park.

28   *TravelTrade*, 28 October 1992, p. 10.

29   Connie S. Sawyer, General Manager, Hotel Iroquois, 49 West 44th Street, New York, in a letter to the author dated 17 December 1993.

30   ibid.

[31] Michael Lee, Federal Minister for Tourism, reported in *The Australian Financial Review*, 11 May 1994, p. 10.

[32] Geoff Carmody, Access Economics, speech to Ninth Australian Tourism Conference, Hobart, 15 October 1993.

[33] *The Australian Financial Review*, 17 August 1994, p. 8.

[34] *The Australian Financial Review*, 31 August 1993, p. 47.

[35] *Cairns and Far North Queensland Tourism Statistical Profile*, prepared for the Far North Queensland Promotion Bureau Ltd by W. S. Cummings Economic Research Services, December 1992, p. 7.

[36] Ron Johnston, Broome Shire President, quoted in *The Australian Financial Review*, 5 January 1993, p. 18.

[37] Cairns City Council, quoted in *Travel and Tourism*, Report No. 423, Industries Assistance Commission, 29 September 1989, p. 183.

[38] The report was undertaken by the National Centre for Studies in Travel and Tourism, in association with R. T. Kinnaird and Associates. It was commissioned by Tourism Training Australia on behalf of the sponsoring group.

[39] Australian Tourism Industry Association, *Special Update*, July 1992.

[40] *The Age*, 5 August 1992, p. 6.

[41] Jennifer Craik, *Resorting to Tourism: Cultural Policies for Tourist Development in Australia*, Allen & Unwin, Sydney, 1991, p. 11.

[42] Industries Assistance Commission, *Travel and Tourism*, Report No. 423, 29 September 1994, p. 140.

[43] ibid., p. 155.

[44] ibid., Table J6, p. J18. 'Restaurants, Hotels and Clubs' is the only ABS labour force classification for the hospitality industry.

[45] *The Catering Institute: A Membership Guide*, proof copy, 1994.

[46] The table is reproduced from Table J6 in the IAC report. The 1994 figures were calculated from Table 47, Employed persons: occupation of full-time and part-time workers, May 1994, *The Labour Force, Australia*, ABS Cat. No. 6203.0.

[47] National Restaurant and Catering Association estimate. By no means all people in the business are members.

[48] Building Owners and Managers Association, *Tourism Development Survey*, p. 1. The number of establishments was correct at January 1994; the number of employees in three-to-five-star hotels was correct at December 1990.

[49] Martin Ferguson, ACTU President, reported in *The Australian Financial Review*, 10 August 1993, p. 48.

[50] As at August 1994.

[51] ABS, *The Labour Force, Australia*, Cat. No. 6203.0, May 1994. The ABS figures do not match those which came directly from the personnel departments of Qantas and Ansett. The ABS compiles its figures from household surveys and believes they could be understated because people in certain jobs (e.g. cleaners) may not always identify themselves with air transport. It is important to retain the ABS figures in this part of the chapter because of their relativity with figures for other forms of transport which come from the same source.

[52] ibid. The road figures specify passenger transport, railways and water transport include freight services.

[53] ABS, *1993 Directory of Transport Statistics*, Cat. No. 1132.0.

[54] Australian Pacific Tours and AAT-King's are more properly described as tour operators. They do operate large numbers of coaches, but the focus of both companies is on devising, marketing and operating tours.

[55] *The Sunday Age*, 21 August 1994, Agenda 9.

[56] This was the situation in September 1994, but it was changing fast. After buying the National Australia Bank and Westpac chains, then Thomas Cook's corporate travel business, American Express was reorganising. This was affecting the number of agencies it owned, while it was increasing its franchising operation. Jetset was also increasing its franchised and associated agency groupings.

[57] Interview with Billee Boyd, General Manager of Wilshire James Travel, 16 February 1993.

[58] Interview with Robin Amos, Australian Services Union, 19 August 1994.

[59] See Note 51. However, the company's origins may be traced to Melbourne suburban bus operations.

60 His successors have done his name proud: in 1994 American Express bought one division of the business which bears his name, Corporate Travel Management Services (worldwide) for $500 million.

61 *TravelTrade Year Book*, January–June 1994.

62 The casino companies are big employers. Jupiters on the Gold Coast, which includes the Conrad Hilton Hotel, has more than 2000 employees.

63 *Amusement and Theme Parks, Australia, 1991–92*, Cat. No. 8675.0, released July 1994.

64 *The Weekend Australian*, 30 April–1 May 1994, p. 6.

65 Interview, Australian Duty Free Operators' Association, 5 July 1994.

66 *The Age*, 5 August 1992, classified feature.

67 Department of Tourism and Queensland Tourist and Travel Corporation figures are staff ceilings; ATC numbers are at 30 June 1993 and include 42 people locally engaged in overseas offices. South Australian figures omit nine people employed interstate as of August 1994, who were to be replaced by consultants. Tasmanian figures are for the tourism component of the Department of Tourism, Sport and Recreation and do not include anyone from the Department's administration.

68 These definitions are adapted from a speech by Wayne Kayler-Thomson, President, Country Victoria Tourism Council, to the Australian Tourism Conference, Hobart, October 1993.

69 Graham Wackett, Chief Executive, Southern Pacific Hotel Corporation, quoted in *Business Review Weekly*, 17 April 1992, p. 38.

70 He is the manager of the yield management department, dealing with fares and schedules, and he needs people with proven analytical ability.

71 *ATIA Special Update*, July 1992.

72 The information in the table is taken from a report in *The Australian*, 19 September 1994, quoting Don Beresford, a former director of the New South Wales Tourism Department, who was conducting the survey for the Office of Multicultural Affairs and the Inbound Tourism Organisation of Australia.

Investment

Putting faith into the future

TOPICS

- What investment means
- Needs by sector
- Who owns the big assets
- Where money comes from
- Where money does not come from
- The Stock Exchange Tourism and Leisure Index

Risky business

ABOUT THIS CHAPTER

Investment provides the means to expand travel and tourism, but it also means taking risks with money. Collectively, investment on a huge scale is required to sustain our travel and tourism industry and allow it to grow. This chapter defines investment and then looks at samples of the requirements in some of the major sectors.

What investment means

Investment usually means putting money into an enterprise to start it up or to expand it. In Big Picture tourism it involves big money, billions of dollars for roads, airports, hotels, resorts and theme parks. In Enterprise tourism it may mean investment through the Stock Exchange for a major project; or personal borrowing from a bank, using savings or mortgaging a house to start a city restaurant, a rainforest tour operating business or a suburban travel agency. It means having faith in the future.

Investment means tying money up—it is no longer available to buy food or to pay for a holiday or a new car. It means taking a risk. The longer the investment is expected to take before providing a return, the greater the risk. Consider the investment in a new hotel: it may be three years or even five before the property is built, marketed and operating. Conditions expected in the feasibility study may have changed radically by then.

The 1980s provided examples of high investment and high risk in tourism plant, particularly in hotels and resorts. The early 1990s showed who reaped the benefits; in most cases it was not the original investors. Far from providing the investors with benefits, billions were lost and some people were ruined. Among those who lost heavily on tourism projects were companies led by people who were known throughout Australia, such as Alan Bond and Christopher Skase.

But did the *nation* lose? Some of the building of hotel and resort complexes in the 1980s was ill-advised; the projects were in the wrong place or not the best concept for the location. Nevertheless, other projects took Australia to a higher level as an international attraction. The Mirage resorts are an example.

It is also true that, while the original investors lost heavily, new owners were able to buy at prices that allowed them to operate properties profitably at rates which were competitive with those in other destinations. This may be thought of as a way of keeping us competitive, cruel but effective. However, that is a short-term view, since no one would invest in the first place if he or she thought that was the usual sequence of events. It would be foolish to think that the financial failures of the 1980s have not had a net overall bad effect on prospects for the 1990s.

The need for investment

Catering for a vast movement of people requires vast investment. The World Travel & Tourism Council estimates that in 1994 investment in new facilities for travel and tourism around the world amounted to $US693 billion, or 10.7 per cent of total investment. This was enough to accommodate 24 million long-term jobs.

Think of the ubiquitous Boeing 747, flown internationally by both Qantas and Ansett and many of the international carriers flying to Australia. A new 400 series jumbo costs around $US130 million. When 747s and other planes bring visitors to Australia, the facilities and services must be in place or the visitor flow will soon dry up. Australian travellers must also be catered for. Put the two together, continue to expand the aggregate and increase expectations and the result is a continuous and rising demand for investment.

The next part of this chapter gives some idea of what is required under these headings:

- infrastructure
- transport
- accommodation
- food and beverage
- attractions
- travel services
- telecommunications.

This is not an attempt to provide an investment guide or comment on the needs of every possible travel and tourism business. The method chosen is to give examples of the scale of the financial commitment required and indicate what it means for the nation, business enterprises and, to some extent, individuals to provide the resources for a large increase in travel and tourism in Australia.

Infrastructure

Infrastructure is the 'hardware', the basic structures that make people movement possible: air and sea ports, roads and railway lines, bridges, water supply, sewerage reticulation and so on. Most of it is provided by public authorities on behalf of the community or the population-at-large, and serves other needs as well as those of travel and tourism.

In the case of international airports, the Commonwealth Government at first simply provided them, except for Cairns.[1] Later it sought to reduce the cost to the public purse by creating a statutory authority (the Federal Airports Corporation) to run them as a business organisation. Then it was announced that Federal Cabinet had approved a plan to 'sell' the 22 airports run by the Corporation to private interests through long-term leases that would ensure the Government still retained ultimate control. Estimates of revenue from the leasing varied between $1647 million and $2287 million.[2]

Meanwhile, the Corporation was proceeding with its capital works program to improve and expand airport facilities. This is costed at $1.6 billion, of which $283 million was spent in 1994. The third runway at Sydney's Kingsford Smith Airport was completed during that year. It cost $250 million. An underground rail link in Sydney between the city and the airport, to be built in time for the 2000 Olympics, will cost $470 million and a railway linking Parramatta with the city, announced at much the same time, will cost another $400 million.[3]

In Australia roads, even more fundamental to travel than airports, win the prize for infrastructure expenditure. The bill for a single bypass, skirting Wangaratta on the Hume Freeway, was $85 million. The three levels of government in Australia spend more than $5 billion a year on roads (see Table 13.1).

Table 13.1   Government spending on roads, 1991–92

Item	Commonwealth	State	Local	Total
	$m	$m	$m	$m
Street lighting			157.1	157.1
Road construction	9.0	2 039.0	991.7	3 039.7
Road maintenance		1 088.0	1 097.2	2 185.2
TOTALS	9.0	3 127.0	2 246.0	5 382.0

Source: ABS — *1993 Directory of Transport Statistics*, Cat. No. 1132.0

On the world scene airport costs are troubling airlines, which ultimately bear much of those costs in landing and other charges. When the city of Osaka needed a new airport, the Japanese decided to build it five kilometres offshore in Osaka Bay to avoid noise pollution and other problems. The site was empty ocean, 18 metres deep. So they built an artificial island of 511 hectares, which took five years and 180 million cubic metres of landfill. Massive subsidence delayed the project by 18 months and caused a cost over-run of $7 billion. The final cost for the airport, which opened in September 1994, was put at $20 billion.[4]

Hong Kong's new Chek Lap Kok airport program is made up of 10 linked infrastructure projects including 34 kilometres of new highways, a railway, reclaimed land and a new town as well as the airport itself. It is one of the world's largest projects, estimated to cost $28 billion, and is scheduled for completion in 1997.[5]

Not surprisingly, governments round the world are avoiding direct investment in airports and insisting that private enterprise bear most of the costs. Eventually, the user pays.

> . . . what airlines have failed to take into account is that the days when airports were simply provided by governments have gone. In these days of fiscal austerity, governments expect airports to pay for themselves—and often, the airport authorities have taken out commercial loans from financial institutions which expect an immediate return once the airport opens.[6]

The principle of private companies providing infrastructure which governments would have paid for in another era has extended beyond airports themselves. The Victorian Premier has said that a number of companies are prepared to build an airport link to the city of Melbourne. The proposals include heavy rail, monorail and O-bahn bus options and range in cost from $150 million to $500 million.[7]

Transport

We have seen already that a Boeing 747-400 costs around $US130 million (see page 126). The Boeing 737 is the workhorse of the Australian domestic air fleets. In June 1992, the Australian airlines were flying 41 of them. The most common variant, the 737-300, costs $US32 million.

Passenger ships are also expensive, but two known to Australians were cheaper than a 747: the 31 000-tonne ferry *Spirit of Tasmania* cost the Tasmanian Government about $US120 million, while Cunard's handsome cruise ship *Crown Monarch* (now withdrawn from Australian service) was built for $US90 million.

As for land vehicles, a popular single-deck 45-seat touring coach costs about $450 000. The Australian Bus and Coach Association says the assets of the members of its affiliates, who represent 95 per cent of private operators, are around $1.5 billion, including $700 million invested in buses and coaches.

A typical year's imports bill for transport equipment is an indicator of the investment required. In 1991–92, imports of transport equipment totalled $7772 million, 15 per cent of the cost of all Australia's imports that year. Of this, road vehicles accounted for nearly 62 per cent while aircraft and parts accounted for a further 27 per cent (see Table 13.2).

Table 13.2   Imports of transport equipment, 1991–92

Road vehicles	$'000	Other transport	$'000
Passenger vehicles	2 553 062	Aircraft	1 580 333
Public transport vehicles	52 948	Railway/tramway vehicles	3 970
Motor cycles	116 984	Marine vehicles	296 629
Other vehicles	1 097 079	Transport equipment parts	618 289
Caravans, trailers etc.	17 411	TOTAL	2 499 221
Vehicle parts	970 985		
TOTAL	4 808 469	Tyres	464 919

Source: ABS — *1993 Directory of Transport Statistics*, Cat. No. 1132.0

Accommodation

At the top end of the accommodation scale, the cost of a hotel or resort is in the hundreds of millions. Sydney's 560-room Park Grand Hotel and an adjoining office block cost its developers $650 million. When an offer of $300 million was made for the hotel, the agents described it as 'absurdly low'. It was sold to the American company ITT-Sheraton for 'about $310 million'.[8] During the exuberant expansion of the 1980s, the five biggest investors in hotels—AGC/Westpac, Beneficial Finance/State Bank of South Australia, Tricontinental/State Bank of Victoria, Long Term Credit Bank of Japan and Daikyo—spent $7 billion.

The quantity surveyors, Rider Hunt Melbourne Pty Ltd,[9] list the following costs as a guide to building multi-storey hotels in Melbourne.

Classification	$ per bedroom
Five-star	180 000–240 000
Four-star	130 000–170 000
Three-star	70 000–120 000
All suites	130 000–160 000

These figures are just for the building: they exclude the cost of land, site works and drainage, basements and car-parking, loose furniture and fittings.

Food and beverage

Some restaurants cost millions, but a survey of 50 restaurants for the National Restaurant and Catering Association in 1990 suggested likely investment in a mid-size restaurant was about $300 000–400 000. Fit-out for a mid-size restaurant (say 125 square metres) would be about $150 000 excluding decorative items, tables and chairs. Fit-out for a typical food court shop would cost about $200 000 and for a coffee shop $80 000.[10]

Attractions

Constructed attractions come in great variety, from those with an educational purpose, like heritage parks, to those that are pure entertainment, like Movie World or casinos.

The latter give us our examples of the big spending sometimes necessary to attract tourists. Movie World was a $120-million item when it opened on the Gold Coast. Melbourne's Crown Casino complex, which will include a 1000-room hotel and a convention centre with a capacity for 3000 delegates, is expected to cost nearly $900 million. The total investment required for building casinos announced in 1994—in Melbourne, Sydney, Cairns, Brisbane and on Christmas Island—was close to $2.5 billion.

Victoria's new museum is to cost $250 million, funded by the Government's revenue from the Crown Casino.

Travel services

Examples of businesses in the travel service category are tour operators, travel agents, tour guides, conference organisers and incentive travel houses. The investment required is not so great, because these companies use people and communications systems to make their money rather than expensive vehicles or buildings.

Nevertheless, the largest of them, Jetset Tours Pty Ltd, is one of Australia's biggest private companies. At the end of the 1993 financial year, shareholders' funds were slightly less than $36 million and total assets were $98.5 million.[11]

There are about 200 Jetset travel locations around Australia. Most of them are franchised; 10 per cent are wholly owned by Jetset. The franchisees are independent owner-operators who pay an initial $25 000 franchise fee to Jetset. This entitles them to the use of the name, external signage, the Worldmaster computer system, marketing and other services. Jetset spends about $5 million a year on television and press advertising focused on Jetset travel locations. A new Jetset travel agency costs about $125 000 to start up.

Other franchises are cheaper, and it might be cheaper still to set up an independent agency. However, to get a licence requires a substantial contribution to the Travel Compensation Fund and, considering the competition and the cost of systems, the days of setting up an agency 'for the cost of a used car'[12] seem to be over.

Telecommunications

Computers and telecommunications technology are very much part of the travel and tourism scene.

The world's airlines have built their own international data network through the Société Internationale de Télécommunications Aéronautiques (SITA). It is now not only a co-operative providing communications services to the airline industry, but also one that provides facilities for other industries.

SITA has a particularly important role in Australia because it supplies the communications network for TIAS (Travel Industries Automated Systems); and TIAS provides the platform for the two major central reservations systems, Sabre and Galileo. An estimated 4000 travel agents use the two systems in Australia and New Zealand. TIAS is owned by Air New Zealand, Ansett Airlines and Qantas. The contract with SITA is worth about $60 million over the five years until the end of the century.

SITA's investment to create the world's largest international data network is estimated at $US1 billion. The world-wide investment in Sabre is $US1.3 billion and in Galileo $US1.5 billion.[13]

Names can be deceiving

Companies with famous brand-names are not necessarily the owners of the expensive assets with which they are identified. Here are some examples:

- The Qantas 747 you see at the airport most likely belongs to a bank or leasing company. Airlines usually lease their aircraft, paying a fee of about 1.5 per cent of the total cost per month.
- The owners of Ansett Airlines, News Corporation and TNT have their own aircraft leasing company, Ansett World Aviation Services, which operates all over the world. The 747s Ansett Airlines flies internationally are leased from Singapore Airlines.
- The big rent-a-car companies—Avis, Budget, Hertz, Delta and Thrifty—lease their cars, usually from the manufacturers and sometimes from dealers.
- Hilton Hotels of Australia Pty Ltd owns the Adelaide Hilton, but the owners of the Sydney Hilton are from Hong Kong, the Melbourne Hilton On The Park from Singapore and the Perth Parmelia Hilton from Malaysia. By and large, the best-known hotels are not owned by the hotel management companies that operate them. The big chains—Sheraton, Radisson, Hyatt, Hilton, Southern Pacific and so on—usually work under a contract with the owner.

There are exceptions. We have seen that Hilton bought its Adelaide hotel and Sheraton bought the Park Grand in Sydney. The Australian Tourism Group (which trades under the Country Comfort name) is the biggest hotel owner in the country in terms of number of properties (27 owned and managed). The Accor Asia Pacific group, which operates under a number of brands including Novotel and Ibis, has been a big buyer of Australian properties. Southern Pacific Hotel Corporation has declared its intention to take part-equity in hotels or participate in joint ventures to develop hotels.[14]

CHAPTER 14

Sources of funds

ABOUT THIS CHAPTER

Funds come from a variety of sources, big and small. There are difficulties in attracting money from some of the more logical sources, and this chapter examines the reasons as well as recent initiatives to give institutional investors more reliable information on which they can base judgements. Foreign investors have been prominent since the 1980s. The criteria of institutions which will invest, and the requirements for the smaller business, are treated in some detail.

A mixed bag

Where does the money come from to provide the facilities that make travel and tourism possible? A 1992 study made by chartered accountants Ernst & Young for the Australian Tourism Industry Association (now the Tourism Council Australia) gave this breakdown for 1989–90:

	%
financial institutions	25
public companies	18
foreign investors	18
private investors	38

However, the study pointed out that there were fluctuations from year to year and that in 1991 foreign investment provided 44 per cent of new expenditures.[15]

This section looks at the investment scene under these headings:

- the three levels of government
- financial institutions

- public companies
- foreign investors
- private investors
- specialist sources
- banks and the small investor.

The three levels of government

All three levels of government are involved in providing public infrastructure such as roads, ports, sewerage plants, water supply and so on. They raise the money by taxes and by borrowing.

Sometimes, they feel compelled to take a more central role in plant development, as when the Northern Territory Government financed the building of the Yulara Resort complex near Ayers Rock. The four-hotel complex now known as the Ayers Rock Resort is reported to have cost the Northern Territory Government more than $500 million. To meet a requirement of the Loan Council, at the end of 1993 the Government sold 40 per cent of the property for $24 million to an Australian syndicate brought together by the Advent Management Group. The Government has freehold title over the 92-square-kilometre resort.[16]

During the 1980s the Queensland Tourist and Travel Corporation, a statutory authority, acquired Crown land to use as equity in joint ventures following an amendment to an Act of Parliament which enabled the QTTC 'to engage or participate in tourist or travel ventures or development projects'. Parcels of Crown land were vested in the Corporation and these could be used to enter into joint ventures with developers. It was part of the QTTC's strategy to ensure that selected coastal areas had international resorts.

> The most controversial aspect of the QTTC's activities was its joint venture involvement in tourist developments. The first joint venture with Qintex resulted in the construction of the $183 million Sheraton Mirage Resort at Port Douglas, which opened in 1987. The contribution of Crown land to the project netted the corporation $10 million in shares, later realised for $13.5 million.[17]

Financial institutions

Financial insititutions are business entities which hold money balances of individuals or other institutions (or borrow from them) in order to make loans or other investments. Obviously banks are included, but it is usual to distinguish between them and the non-bank financial intermediaries. These include superannuation funds, credit unions, insurance companies, finance companies, building societies and investment trusts.

Because they accumulate huge balances, they are looked upon as the major Australian source of funds for the big tourism projects. However, banks are also the principal source of loan funds for small tourism enterprises. To avoid confusion and because very different issues are involved, that activity will be considered in a separate part of this chapter; here the discussion is confined to major projects.

Financial institutions have not been enthusiastic investors in big projects in the 1990s. A sample of press reports gives these reasons:

- There is a record of bad experience in the 1980s. So many projects failed that the banks were left with massive property inventories which they sold—when they could—at heavy losses. By mid-1993, one in ten of Australia's top-class hotel rooms was in the hands of the banks or receivers; that is, almost 11 000 rooms in 68 hotels of three, four and five stars.[18]
- Accommodation projects are viewed unfavourably against other property investments because of the instability of income. 'Add high operating costs in Australian hotels and resorts, the general fickleness of tourism with weather, fashion and pilots' disputes, plus the poor tax incentives, and you can't blame banks, institutions or individuals for not investing in tourism property.'[19]
- Australian hotels are the fourth least profitable in the world, only bettering Latin America, Mexico and the Caribbean.[20]
- Even when the investment does turn out to be profitable, it takes a long time getting there. A study undertaken by chartered accountants Horwath & Horwath for the Queensland Tourist and Travel Corporation and the Australian Tourism Industry Association found that, on average, hotels did not make a net profit for the first ten years of operation.[21]

The picture is not all negative. There is evidence that building and operating costs in Australia are coming closer to those of competing countries and it is also true that institutions have made selected investments—in the Thakral Property Trust, which part paid for its takeover of Westpac's hotel holdings with a $74 million float on the Australian Stock Exchange; and in the investment in the Ayers Rock Resort led by the Advent Management Group and in support of the Country Comfort Trust (and later the Australian Tourism Group, which replaced it).

> This week the Reef Casino Consortium, in which the Country Comfort group has the largest stake, was awarded the right to develop the $200 million Cairns Casino project.

Backing the bid are about 20 institutional investors, 12 of which already hold stakes in the Country Comfort Trust, plus about eight new players including the big boys Bankers Trust, which is underwriting the float, and MLC, part of the Lend Lease group.

Since Darryl Courtney-O'Connor engineered a $24 million management buy-out of a chain of 12 motel properties that Lend Lease put on the market in 1986, he has been able to attract the backing of institutional investors.[22]

In general, however, institutions are wary or simply not interested.

[Commonwealth Funds Management chief economist Paul] Kelly says the problem for super funds is that the profitability from tourism property or equities has not matched the risk. The instability of income is difficult for managers of defined benefits funds, while tourism investments are typically illiquid. 'We are crying out for a BHP in tourism—a stand-out investment with an air of solidity and a real promise of stable capital and income growth,' Kelly says. 'We need the equivalent of a Hilton or Marriott chain where you can invest in shares that have a spread of hotels and resorts and a proven income stream and the liquidity of trading on the New York stock exchange.

'Instead, most of the offerings are small with little track record, very volatile with not a lot of equity and cashflow.'[23]

The reluctance of institutions to become involved is felt mainly in the accommodation industry, but it has also applied to other enterprises. The Movie World theme park on the Gold Coast was financed by an Asian syndicate because even such established developers as Warner Bros, Sea World and Village Roadshow could not attract Australian capital. The National Australia Bank declined participation, saying that its board of directors had instructed it 'not to consider tourism property'.[24]

Public companies

The economic importance of the Stock Exchange is that it facilitates saving and investment, first through making it possible for investors to dispose of securities quickly if they wish to do so, and secondly by channelling savings into productive investments.

Ready marketability requires that new issues be made or backed by reputable borrowers or institutions, that information be available on existing securities and that there be both a legal framework and market rules to prevent fraud and sharp practices.

Institutions and other big investors usually prefer to put money into companies via the Stock Exchange for these reasons:

- There is reliable published research about the industries in which listed companies operate, the companies' activities and their performances.
- Investment terms are largely controlled by the share price.
- Shares can be traded with relative ease; there is no illiquidity problem with the investment.
- The payment of profits as dividends is open to public scrutiny.

Contrast this with the problems unlisted companies can present investors:

- difficulty of analysis in the investment
- need to negotiate investment terms in detail
- illiquidity of investment
- problems with eventual realisation of profit
- concern over what to do if the investment does not work.

In mid-August 1994 the number of companies in the Australian Stock Exchange's 'tourism and leisure' category was 26 out of a total of 1219 companies listed in all categories. Of these one, Challenger International, a Sydney investment bank, was no longer interested in tourism; another, Mandarin International Ltd, the Hong Kong-based international hotel operator, had its shares on offer through the Exchange but did not operate in Australia; Barrier Reef Holdings had its floating hotel anchored off Ho Chi Minh City; and Islands Hotels Ltd operated hotels in Papua New Guinea and the Solomon Islands.

The other companies can be classified thus.

Hotels, resorts and casinos
Accor Asia Pacific Corporation (AAPC) Ltd, formerly Quality Pacific: hotel owners and managers
Amalgamated Holdings Ltd: hotels, resorts, tour operations
The Ballarat Brewing Company Ltd: hotel, property and share investors
Breakwater Island Trust: owner of Sheraton Breakwater Casino-Hotel (190 rooms) and casino, Townsville
Burswood Property Trust: Burswood Resort hotel (412 rooms) and casino, Perth
Club Crocodile: resort owner and operator
Crown Casino Ltd: Melbourne casino and hotel developer/operator
Hamilton Island Ltd: Queensland resort owner
Jupiters Ltd: owner and operator of a resort complex at Broadbeach on the Gold Coast consisting of the Hotel Conrad (622 rooms), Jupiters casino and a convention centre
Koala Corporation Australia Ltd: operator of hotel properties in Queensland and provider of consulting services to the industry

Port Douglas Reef Resorts: resort and attraction developer/owner
Reef Casino Trust: Cairns casino and hotel owner/developer
Sea World Property Trust: lessor of Sea World entertainment park, 50
    per cent owner of Sea World Nara Resort, owner of $33\frac{1}{3}$ per cent of
    Warner Bros Movie World Joint Venture
Queensland Tourism Industries Ltd: tourism resort and property
    development, financial services and speciality retailing
TAL Holdings Ltd: investment company for Federal Hotels
Thakral Property Trust: hotel owner
Transmetro Ltd: operator of hotels and serviced hotels

Theme parks
Sea World Property Trust (see details under 'Hotels, resorts and
    casinos'): has interests in Sea World entertainment park and Movie
    World Joint Venture
Village Roadshow Ltd: part owner of Movie World; the company is
    also engaged in movie production and distribution
Sydney Aquarium Ltd: owner of the Sydney Aquarium

Transport
Greyhound, Pioneer Australia Ltd: coach operator
Murray River Developments: operator of tourist vessels, shipping
Hazelton Airlines (though not listed in the Exchange's 'tourism and
    leisure' category): this regional airline, established in 1953 by Max
    Hazelton, was once mostly engaged in agricultural work. Now it
    operates to 23 destinations in New South Wales, Victoria,
    Queensland and Tasmania and in 1993 carried 330 000 passengers.

New floats

The Commonwealth Government sold 25 per cent of Qantas Airways in
1993 and intends to float the remaining 75 per cent in 1995.

> Qantas is expected to be valued by the float at between $2.5 billion and $3
> billion, in line with the $655 million price British Airways paid for its 25
> per cent of Qantas last year.
> That means that the new money that will need to be raised from the
> float will be at least $1.9 billion, and possibly more than $2.25 billion.[25]

Between $750 million and $1 billion was expected to be raised from the
public and between $200 million and $250 million from overseas. (There is
to be a limit.) The rest, about $1 billion, was expected from institutions.
    Flight Centres, which owns more travel agencies than any other company
in Australia (142 plus 35 in New Zealand), may float part of the company.

Revenue was $600 million in 1993–94 with a pre-tax profit of $10.4 million. A minimum 20 per cent of the company was to be offered in a float which would primarily be aimed at increasing the level of employee share ownership.[26]

Another high-profile company, Country Comfort Trust Pty Ltd, announced in September 1994 a $200-million public float. The name of the company was changed to Australian Tourism Group, but the hotels it owns and manages continued to trade under the Country Comfort name.

The Australian Tourism Group, which was listed on the Stock Exchange in December 1994; was split between an investment trust, which included the Country Comfort hotels and the Reef Casino Trust investment, and a trading trust, which receives one-third of management fees from external properties.[27]

The Tourism and Leisure Index

The Australian Stock Exchange introduced a Tourism and Leisure Index in mid-1994. There were eight stocks included at the start and others were expected to be added. The Index provides investors with a mechanism for monitoring the included stocks as a group. Importantly, it raises the profile of the classification and is one of a number of initiatives designed to give investors more confidence in travel and tourism.

The establishment in 1993 of the Tourism Forecasting Council, chaired by a leading banker, was a major step forward in providing financiers with data of higher quality. The Council sponsored the creation of the new Index.

The Index is of value to market analysts in institutions and stockbroking firms who track the performance of an industry against the stock market generally and against other industries. Indexes are also used to compare the performance of individual firms against the performance of the industry as a whole.

To be included in the Index, stocks have to meet these criteria:

- The majority of their profits should be sourced from the tourism and leisure industries.
- They should be a constituent of the All Ordinaries Index.
- The company should have a minimum market capitalisation of approximately $60 million.
- They should have a stock turnover of at least 0.5 per cent per month for 3 months.

In July 1994, when it was introduced, the Index represented a market capitalisation of about $3.4 billion.

Table 14.1 shows the initial listings.

Table 14.1 Tourism and Leisure Index, initial listings

Company name	Estimated market capitalisation at 30 June 1994
	$m
Accor Asia Pacific Corporation (AAPC) Ltd	486
Amalgamated Holdings Ltd	156
Burswood Property Trust	686
Crown Casino Ltd	408
Hamilton Island Ltd	114
Jupiters Ltd	724
Sea World Property Trust	233
Village Roadshow Ltd	550
TOTAL	3 357

Source: Australian Stock Exchange, *Forecast*

Foreign investors

Partly because of the reluctance of its institutions to invest in its tourism projects, Australia has been heavily dependent on foreign investment to get them built. In the 1980s, the Japanese were the major investors from overseas, particularly EIE International (backed by the Long Term Credit Bank of Japan), Daikyo, Kajima, Mitsui and Kumagai Gami; there were many other company and individual investors.

However, the downturn in the Japanese lending market combined with recession in Australia saw a massive retreat by Japanese companies. According to one estimate, the six major Japanese developers spent $7 billion on developments in Australia during the 1980s, including tourism projects, and will lose about half of it in the 'bail-out'.[28] One of the six, EIE International, was bankrupted.

Daikyo, the biggest investor in Cairns and one of the biggest on the Gold Coast, made an operating loss of $170 million in 1991, which included write-downs on its $1.3 billion Australian portfolio. It decided to sell its Gold Coast development sites and concentrate on Cairns. In 1992, Daikyo was forced into a restructuring of the group, which included staff cuts and the sale of considerable property, including land and hotel developments in Australia, valued then at $340 million. However, most of the staff cuts and property sales took place in Japan.[29]

The Kajima Corporation wrote off $1 billion in revaluing its Australian properties in 1994. Among the properties it sold were two Sydney hotels, the Radisson Century and Metro Inn. Its restructuring was hampered by a management agreement for its flagship property, the five-star Park Grand in Sydney, and it temporarily put in receivers in a tactical move to remove the managers. This was aimed at saving costs, improving revenue and being able to offer vacant possession to a potential buyer. The property was later sold to ITT Sheraton.

Kumagai Gami, like Kajima a giant construction company, also sold Australian interests including the Observation City hotel in Perth. In 1994 Japanese newspapers reported it would sell $3.8 billion worth of its international real estate holdings within the next five years. But the company also said it would go ahead with a plan to develop a $1-billion integrated resort about 15 kilometres north of Airlie Beach in Far North Queensland in partnership with the merchant bank Wardley James Capel Finance.[30]

Decline in foreign investment

According to the Foreign Investment Review Board, foreign investment in tourism projects declined from $3.9 billion in 1989–90 to $1.3 billion in 1991–92.[31]

A new wave of foreign investment came after this period—not to build, but to buy what others had built and had lost or could not afford to keep. Mostly from South-East Asia, these investors bought at bargain prices. By the end of 1993, two-thirds of the 100 or so hotels with more than 165 rooms in Australia in the three-to-five-star bracket under management agreements were owned by overseas investors.[32] Hotels valued at $800 million had been sold in 1993 alone to investors from:

Singapore	$420m
Malaysia	$114.8m
Hong Kong	$81m
Australia	$78.8m
Indonesia	$30m
others	$69m[33]

In the first three months of 1994, another $145 million of hotel sales were made, 90 per cent to Singapore buyers and the remainder to Australians. By April 1994 the number of quality properties available had dried up and property prices were rising, depressing yields. The Singapore buyers were turning to cheaper markets in the US and Indo-China. The burst of buying in late 1993 and early 1994 was 'driven purely by superior yields here'.[34]

Many landmark hotels changed hands in this intense period of buying. Among them were:

- **to Singapore buyers**
  Sydney—Boulevard, Darling Harbour Parkroyal
  Melbourne—Hilton, Banks, Palm Lake, Eden On The Park, Regency, Bryson

Brisbane—Lennons
Cairns—Palm Cove Travelodge
* **to Malaysian buyers**
Sydney—Rushcutters Bay Travelodge
Perth—Parmelia Hilton
Coffs Harbour—Pelican Beach Travelodge
* **to Hong Kong buyers**
Sydney—Hilton
* **to Indonesian buyers**
Melbourne—Centra On The Yarra.

The biggest investor was Singapore's Thakral Group, which already had an interest in the Menzies Holiday Inn. It bought a package of eight hotels from the Westpac Banking Group, which had become Australia's biggest hotel owner (in value) by default of the original developers. Westpac was reported before the sale to have written down by one-third the value of the properties, which included the Novotel On Collins, Melbourne, and the Darwin Atrium. The price paid by Thakral, $260 million, was the 'price of a single upmarket hotel in Singapore'.[35] Thakral later floated the Thakral Property Trust, raising $74 million from institutions on the Australian Stock Exchange to help pay for the deal.

Perth's five-star Observation City hotel, developed by Alan Bond in 1987 for $70 million, was sold to another Singapore-based investment group for $48 million. It was said to have a replacement value of $140 million.[36]

Generally, the investors got bargains. Table 14.2 shows how four Melbourne four-star hotels were sold at far less than replacement cost. Their sale price is compared with Rider Hunt's estimated building costs given in Chapter 13 (pages 129–30). The range of building costs has been averaged to $150 000 per bedroom; suites have been counted as rooms; no allowance has been made for land, furniture, fittings, basements or parking. All four were sold for less than the replacement cost of their bricks and mortar.

In non-property fields, foreign interests are also prominent. British Airways owns a quarter of Qantas Airways; Air New Zealand owns half

Table 14.2 Hotel sales and replacement costs, 1993–94

Hotel	Number of rooms/suites	Sale price	Replacement cost of building only
		$m	$m
Eden On The Park	132	16	19.8
Bryson	363	50	54.5
Banks	204	22	30.1
Centra On The Yarra	397	52.5	59.6

Sources: Newspapers; *Riders Digest*, 1993; RACV — *A–Z Australian Accommodation Guide*, 1994–95 edition

of Jetset; the Helicopter Line of New Zealand controls prominent wholesale tour operators World Travel Headquarters, Newmans Holidays and Travel-marvel; and American Express is one of Australia's biggest travel retailers.

Does it matter if foreigners own some of our most important travel and tourist assets? In 1991 a report titled *Impacts of Foreign Investment in Australian Tourism*, jointly funded by the Commonwealth and Queensland Governments, concluded that there are net benefits to Australia from foreign investment in the travel and tourism industry and that Australia can maximise gains from tourism by adopting a liberal policy towards foreign investment.

> A significant finding of the report is that there is very little difference between the impact on the economy of domestic and foreign investment in tourism. This is because the economic impact is not so much dependent on ownership of facilities as on the sources of inputs to facilities, and most of the inputs used in foreign-owned facilities (labour, construction materials, foods and cleaning services etc) are domestically sourced.[37]

Private investors

Given the nature of the travel and tourism business structure and the small number of publicly listed companies involved, private investment is a very important source of funds.

Private investors provide the bulk of capital needed for the smaller businesses (and remember, there are more than 100 000 of them): the smaller hotels, motels, guest houses, recreational facilities, coach companies, car services, restaurants, souvenir shops, travel agents, tour services and so on.

Many small businesses are started on savings, a mortgage on a house or borrowings from relatives. Sometimes capital is raised from individual investors through an intermediary—a lawyer, accountant, merchant banker or other financial adviser—who has a client or clients with a liking for a particular kind of investment.

Two specialist sources

Here we shall look in some detail at two organisations—the Advent Management Group and the Commonwealth Development Bank—which are particularly important in travel and tourism investment, not only because they are willing investors but also because of the standards they set in assessing investment prospects.

The Advent Management Group

In contrast to other investors, the Advent Management Group has researched the travel and tourism sector and found a 'significant number of well-run, growing and profitable businesses'. It attracts institutional investors to its Advent Tourism Development Fund, which it then invests in quality businesses.

Noted for the thoroughness of their examination of prospective businesses, the Advent Tourism Development Fund managers have a successful track record of investing in a range of businesses from tour operations to theme parks, and from cruise operations to accommodation.

In a document prepared in late 1993 for prospective investors, the Advent Management Group states: 'There are an increasing number of experienced, professional operational managers being attracted to the tourism, leisure and hospitality industry and this is changing the culture of business in this sector to be profit rather than lifestyle driven.'

Advent looks for these five criteria in an investment proposal:

- **Management** It believes the strength of the management team is the most important consideration in the investment decision. The team should be experienced in the industry in which the business competes, must have a thorough knowledge of its market and have a well-thought-out strategy for development.
- **Market** The market in which the business operates should have superior long-term growth prospects and be big enough for the business to achieve a significant base of sales.
- **Competitive advantage** The product or service should be sufficiently unusual to enjoy sustainable competitive advantages which will enable it to enjoy above-average profitability.
- **Barriers to entry** Competitive advantages should represent a barrier to entry by competitors and give an investor confidence in the sustainability of a company's performance.
- **Financial return** Advent's objective is to earn a rate of return of at least 25 per cent in each new investment.

Advent conducts a rigorous examination of each prospect, going through these steps:

1 A filter process is carried out, dealing with general operations to see if the investment will fit the fund strategy. Does the company meet the criteria? Can Advent work with the management company?
2 The prospect is then examined to see if there is a reason why Advent should not invest.
3 If it is still in play, it is submitted to the investment committee.
4 Following the committee's approval, it is submitted to the board of directors for a final decision.

Advent accepts about 3 per cent of the deals it examines. As a general rule, it is not interested in start-up or early stage businesses because typically they have little or no revenue, narrow product ranges and new management teams.[38]

The Commonwealth Development Bank

However, the Commonwealth Development Bank will look at start-up as well as operating companies and has been established to help enterprises, mainly small to medium-sized businesses, which have difficulty finding finance because:

- the security available may not be enough to support the sum needed to be borrowed
- a long term may be necessary for repayment
- the enterprise may be about to start up and therefore does not have a track record; or it may be operating but does not yet have a sound track record
- the financial backing for the business may be weak.

The Commonwealth Development Bank will examine these situations and, if it is satisfied that the enterprise is commercially viable, will help provide a financial package.

It does not compete with other banks; in fact, its customers usually approach their own banks first and are then referred to the Commonwealth Development Bank. A number of banks act as its agents.

Besides loan funds, the Commonwealth Development Bank can provide equity finance—capital investment—for small and medium-sized businesses that can demonstrate prospects of strong sales and profit growth. At 30 June 1993, the Commonwealth Development Bank had outstanding loans to tourism projects totalling $115 351 000 in these categories:

caravan parks	$17 611 000
motels and hotels	$62 105 000
resorts and recreation	$24 558 000
tourist attractions	$11 077 000[39]

Banks and the small investor

Many small tourism businesses start with not much more than a spirit of enterprise, pluck, some savings and family help. However, none should be started without taking these steps:

- Consulting a small business organisation. There is one in every State. As an example, Small Business Victoria has a tourism facilitator for individual consultation. It also has a valuable bookshop with specific tourism publications as well as those relating to running a small business generally; it runs seminars and other activities intended to develop management skills.
- Obtaining a copy of *The Business of Tourism* from the Australian Bankers' Association; this is a financial management guide for tourism-based businesses, produced by the Association in conjunction with the Commonwealth Department of Tourism and the Financial Management Research Centre.

The Business of Tourism is an important document. As an example of its common-sense approach, it has this to say about the 'perceptions of tourism':

> One of the measures of the success of our tourism industry is in the number of 'movements' whether 'in-bound' or domestic tourists each year. In recent years, Australia's performance has been very strong in generating tourist traffic.
>
> Another indicator, and a particularly relevant one in a private-enterprise dominated sector, is the level of profitability of the businesses which comprise the 'industry'. On this measure, Australian tourism is not as healthy as the visitor numbers might indicate. The industry is plagued by low profitability and a high turnover in the number of operators moving in and out of business.
>
> It cannot be forgotten that tourism is dominated by small business operators. Research over a long period of time has demonstrated the high risk of failure in small business—about 80% of new businesses fail within five years of their establishment. So many tourism businesses, by virtue of being 'small businesses' are prone to a high failure rate. This is only exacerbated by the seasonal nature of many tourism-based businesses.
>
> One of the most fundamental changes needed to improve and reconcile these different perceptions is for 'tourism' businesses to become more profitable. This financial management guide aims to help this process, particularly by concentrating on:
> - how to establish suitable levels of debt for a business;
> - how to deal in an effective way with bank personnel; and
> - how to manage the business in a professional way.

This publication is organised as a workbook, with checklists, examples and case studies in its 214 folio-sized pages. Its section headings are: Preparing Yourself, Establishing a Business Using Borrowed Money, Effective Business Management, Investing in Relationships for Business Survival, and Industry Briefings.

Here is a selection of quotes from *The Business of Tourism*:

Borrowing money is a fact of commercial life. Borrowing too much money threatens the survival of the business; borrowing too little money can often stunt its growth and development.

A satisfactory investment—from the point of view of the tourism operator and the banker—is one which promises to return more than enough to repay the initial loan plus the interest associated with the loan. So, the viability of any borrowing depends on:

- the interest rate applying to the debt;
- the likely rate of return on assets employed in the project—this includes the expected operating or trading profits plus anticipated capital gains; and
- the risks associated with the project.

Many business operators seem to expect a banker to have a detailed knowledge of all the factors involved in a particular business or industry sector. Discussions with a number of operators revealed that almost one-third of them felt that their banker's knowledge was 'poor'; by comparison, only 5% of bankers thought their sector-specific knowledge was 'poor'.

In the discussions carried out, bankers generally rated the financial aspects of their dealings with customers as less satisfactory than the operators did. For example, about 20% of bankers rated the quality of loan proposals as 'good' or 'very good', while 60% of operators felt that their proposals were either 'good' or 'very good'.

When determining how much to borrow, it is advisable to be conservative in estimating your expected income and generous in estimating your expenses. Your estimates should be done on two different bases—the 'most likely' and a 'worst case' scenario. The important point to remember is that each bank or lender will place its emphasis on different indicators, and will have different opinions about what is a 'satisfactory' result.

It is important when making a loan application to view it from the lender's point of view.

You must have and must demonstrate confidence that you can manage the business profitably, and cope with any unforeseen circumstances that may arise. You will only have this confidence after a thorough analysis of your prospects.

One consideration often overlooked in establishing a business is the length of time taken to generate reasonable profits. In its very early days, the business may trade at a loss, or only generate low levels of profit. At the same time, however, you will be investing in equipment, building up stock or debtor levels, and spending relatively large amounts on promotion and advertising. During this period, you may need to rely on another source of cash or income (e.g., a supportive family; some form of part-time employment which does not prevent you from operating the business; or a pre-arranged line of credit).

Growth should be sought for the right reasons:
- the capacity to offer a more complete service to customers;
- the better use of resources and the achievement of higher profits; or
- to provide extra challenges for the owners and staff of the business.

Any asset used in a tourism-based business will be worked hard by your customers. Whether the asset is a building, or a piece of furniture or a vehicle, it will be in regular use and may be treated more harshly than your customers would treat their own belongings. Maintaining the quality of assets is essential to the long-term success of the business; maintenance must be planned for. This planning includes assessing the cashflow impact and making sure that suitable time is available to perform the maintenance.

Your capital purchases should be determined by three questions:
- Do we need it?
- Do we need it now?
- Does it have to cost that much?

All businesses operate in an uncertain environment. Planning for the future incorporates elements of risk and uncertainty. Ensuring that the business is well-located, offers products or services which are in genuine demand, is appropriately financed and well managed will ensure its survival.

Many businesses don't plan to fail—they simply fail to plan.

NOTES ON SECTION 5

[1] There were 395 licensed airports in Australia in June 1992, of which 11 were international airports. The majority of licensed aerodromes were owned and operated by local councils, State government departments and private companies. The remaining 65 aerodromes were owned and operated by the Federal Airports Corporation (which owned 22), the Department of Defence or the Department of Transport and Communications.

[2] The merchant bank Barclays de Zoete Wedd estimated the sale would bring $2248 million if the airports were sold individually and $2287 million if sold in 'clusters' (several small airports with one big one). The FAC estimated the airports would bring $1647 million if sold individually and $1718 million if sold in clusters. These figures were based on the intention to sell the airports outright, not lease them.

[3] *Weekend Australian*, 6 August 1994, p. 8.

[4] *Herald Sun*, 4 August 1994, p. 45.

[5] *The Australian Financial Review*, 17 August 1994, p. 42.

[6] *Airline Business* (UK), May 1994, p. 5.

[7] *Herald Sun*, 4 August 1994, p. 29.

[8] *Weekend Australian*, 4 August 1994, Property 6.

[9] *Riders Digest*, 1993.

10 Rider Hunt Melbourne Pty Ltd, interview July 1994.

11 *Herald Sun*, 15 January 1994, p. 21.

12 A statement attributed to John Dart, Executive Director of the Australian Federation of Travel Agents.

13 Statistics supplied by SITA.

14 *Weekend Australian*, 24–25 September 1994, Property 1.

15 Supplementary Report from Ernst & Young to the Australian Tourism Industry Association on Investment in the Tourism Industry, 11 February 1992.

16 *Herald Sun*, 1 January 1994, p. 24.

17 Jennifer Craik, *Resorting to Tourism: Cultural Policies for Tourist Development in Australia*, Allen & Unwin, Sydney, 1991, p. 189.

18 *The Australian Financial Review*, 4 June 1993, p. 48.

19 *Business Review Weekly*, 19 June 1992, p. 32, quoting Ross Woods, Director of tourism and property consultants Horwath & Horwath Services.

20 *Weekend Australian*, 23–24 July 1994, Property 1. It attributed the information to a Horwath Asia Pacific analysis.

21 *The Age*, 30 September 1993, p. 19.

22 *The Australian Financial Review*, 29 July 1993, p. 38. The newspaper said that Mr Courtney-O'Connor had succeeded with institutional investors where others had been spurned because of his 'ability to deliver steadily rising profits—from $3.1 million ($5100 a room) for the year to June 1987 to an estimated $16 million for the year to June 1993 ($9550 a room)'.

23 'Why Banks Won't Invest', *Business Review Weekly*, 14 February 1992, pp. 18–21.

24 ibid.

25 Stephen Bartholomeusz, financial columnist, *The Age*, 1 September 1994, p. 21. The price British Airways paid for its share of Qantas was actually $665 million.

26 *The Australian*, 21 September 1994, p. 48.

27 *The Australian*, 23 September 1994, p. 20.

28 *Weekend Australian*, 19–20 February 1994, p. 20.

29 *Weekend Australian*, 3–4 October 1992, p. 34.

30 *Weekend Australian*, 19–20 March 1994, Property 1.

31 Annual reports of the Foreign Investment Review Board, 1990–91, p. vi and 1991–92, p. 3.

32 Australian Hospitality International survey, unpublished, March 1994.

33 Colliers Jardine survey quoted in the *Weekend Australian*, 23–24 April 1994, Property 2.

34 *Weekend Australian*, 30 April–1 May 1994, p. 33.

35 *Weekend Australian*, 26–27 March 1994.

36 *The Australian Financial Review*, 22 February 1994, p. 48.

37 *Tourism—Australia's Passport to Growth: A National Tourism Strategy*, Commonwealth Department of Tourism, June 1992, p. 29.

38 Notes taken during an interview with Ronald S. Finkel, Director—Investments, Advent Management Group, 5 November 1993.

39 Commonwealth Development Bank information booklet.

Planning for the future

Forecasting and common sense

TOPICS

- Accommodation concerns
- The Tourism Forecasting Council examined
- The first domestic forecasts
- The first international forecasts
- The regions as a key to national planning
- Consolidation of government agencies
- Co-operation with the States

CHAPTER 15

The accommodation challenge

ABOUT THIS CHAPTER

Having enough accommodation to meet future growth is the biggest worry for Big Picture planners. As the economy recovered in the mid-1990s, confidence returned, but there was no early sign that there would be sufficient investment in new buildings in time to cater for the expected volume of tourism at about the end of the century.

Predicted shortages

The challenge for Australia is to provide enough suitable accommodation for the future growth of tourism. This is expected to be so rapid that, even though as this is written there is excess capacity in most categories, shortages are expected in the mid-1990s in Brisbane, the Gold Coast, Far North Queensland, Darwin and Perth and generally elsewhere by the end of the century—that is, unless there is substantial new construction. Because of the extra requirement for Sydney as a result of the Olympic Games, Tourism New South Wales has suggested the city will need up to 15 new hotels or an extra 8000 rooms to meet demand in 2000.

There were 47 new accommodation projects of at least three-star standard under way in 1994, according to the Building Owners and Managers Association (BOMA), and more to come including Australia's biggest, the 1000-room hotel to be built as part of Melbourne's Crown Casino project.

BOMA provided the summary of new developments shown in Table 15.1. If the 'mooted' total becomes actuality it will still be short of the minimum requirement predicted for 2000 in the Commonwealth Department of Tourism's 1992 document entitled *Tourism—Australia's Passport to Growth: A National Tourism Strategy*. Based on high and low scenario growth rates for

Table 15.1   New accommodation developments, 1994

	Total	1994	1995	1996	1997+	Mooted
Number of projects	63	47	10	4	2	283
Number of bedrooms	4 137	1 812	669	936	720	15 514
Investment value ($m)	1 433.4	250.9	269.2	104.3	809.0	n.a.
% foreign investment	4.6	15.0	–	27.4	–	n.a.

Source: BOMA, July 1994

inbound and domestic tourism in 1992, this publication estimated that between 30 000 and 90 000 new hotel and motel rooms would need to be built.

An Ernst & Young study in 1991 estimated that by 2000 there would be a need to provide an additional 96 000 hostel beds, 62 000 caravan sites and 43 000 holiday units.

> My concern is that financiers and governments will realise Australia needs a lot more tourism capacity when existing hotels and resorts are bulging and tourists are being turned away. Then we'll have a rush. It takes three years to get concept plans approved by local government and years more to get something built.
>
> We'll be five or six years behind demand.[1]

Two years after that statement was made, Australia had emerged from recession and the newspapers reflected optimism. Had things changed? The headlines suggested they had: 'Tourism paves way for new wave of hotel investment',[2] 'Investors look to hotels as tourism surges',[3] 'MM's 1995 tourist target'.[1]

However, the 'new wave of tourism investment' was based on an interview with an adviser to Asian investors and the investors who were said to be 'looking' to hotels were also Asian. No projects were mentioned in these or other contemporary reports. Mercantile Mutual's interest was similarly vague:

> I think towards the end of next year we will buy commercial and maybe some three-star tourism accommodation. We are not in agriculture, we are not in tourism . . . the obvious alternative is to invest a small fraction of the fund into something else.[5]

In the second half of 1994 hotel occupancies were rising in most areas, price-cutting was being abandoned and yields were increasing. Increased profitability and a boost in asset values will be the eventual results—better numbers for investors if they are interested. While there is the odd encouraging sign, we still await evidence of a change of heart among institutions.

Tourists need more than accommodation, of course; other elements of the travel and tourism mix have to be provided for the extra demand forecast. Governments usually manage to supply the infrastructure, if not always in time.

Tourism strategic planner Richard Bramley says government must accept that tourism needs coordination to ensure that demand can be met. 'That means government has to get airports to open as new accommodation opens,' he says. 'We've had resorts open with inadequate airports or roads and tour bookings coming through before accommodation and other facilities are ready.'[6]

But it is usually a question of timing rather than supply. At most times, vehicles can be obtained and moved quickly to meet demand. This applies to aircraft, coaches and rental cars; less so to ships.

Accommodation is the big problem. If the Government's 1992 assessment is anywhere near right in its upper-level requirement, then investment of at least that of the 1980s boom will be required. It takes simple arithmetic to work out that even at an average of an extremely modest $100 000 a room, the provision of 90 000 rooms comes to $9 billion, which is probably more than the Japanese invested in new Australian tourism plant in the 1980s. It is hard to imagine that they are ready to do the same in the 1990s.

CHAPTER 16

The Tourism Forecasting Council

ABOUT THIS CHAPTER

Initiatives by the Commonwealth Government have addressed some of the problems associated with investment in travel and tourism in Australia. In particular, the establishment of a Tourism Forecasting Council is most significant. This chapter looks at its composition and first work.

National strategy and actions

The document *Tourism—Australia's Passport to Growth: A National Tourism Strategy* reviewed Australian travel and tourism and in very broad terms set out the things the Commonwealth Government would like to see happen. It was not a strategy in the business sense, setting down the approaches to achieve quantified objectives and providing the basis for an action plan. Indeed, it probably would have been better titled a policy guide. Its value lies in the review material rather than its sense of direction.[7]

Initiatives with positive results were taken by the Commonwealth Government through the Department of Tourism before and after its release, of which two are relevant here:

- *The Business of Tourism* was prepared by the Australian Bankers' Association in conjunction with the Department and released. As the references in Chapter 14 attest (pages 146–8), it is a valuable financial management guide for people in a travel and tourism small business or those thinking of starting or buying one.
- The Tourism Forecasting Council was established; from this followed the Stock Exchange's Tourism and Leisure Index.

The [Tourism Forecasting] Council is a high profile reporting body supported by a technically-oriented advisory body. This structure aims to simultaneously improve both the quality of forecasts and their use by the industry and investment community . . .

Access to finance, including both debt and equity capital, has been identified as a major impediment to the growth of the tourism industry. To help overcome this, the interests of the finance industry and of institutional investors are represented on the Council by the Australian Bankers' Association (ABA), the Life Insurance Federation of Australia (LIFA) and the Building Owners and Managers Association (BOMA).[8]

At its formation, the Council was chaired by a former managing director of Westpac Banking Corporation and its membership included:

the National President of the Australian Hotels Association
the Director of the Bureau of Tourism Research
the Managing Director of the Australian Tourist Commission
the Chairman of the Tourism Council Australia
the Executive Director of the Life Insurance Federation of Australia
the Head of the Tourism Division, Department of Tourism
the Chief Executive Officer of the Building Owners and Managers
  Association
a representative of the Tourism Task Force
the Chairman of the Australian Standing Committee on Tourism
a representative of the Australian Council of Trade Unions
a representative of the Australian Bankers' Association.

Simply gathering these people around a table regularly to talk about tourism is an achievement.

The Council's role

The Council set its first priorities:

- to develop forecasts covering inbound, domestic and outbound tourism movements so that a broader picture of future activity could be developed
- to identify visitor nights and expenditure across those sectors
- to introduce regional forecasts to assist investment planning for accommodation and tourism infrastructure.

Domestic travel forecasts

Technical work began with the first systematic attempt to predict the level of domestic tourism. Non-business travel in Australia (85 per cent of the total) and business travel (15 per cent) were considered separately. These had shown quite different patterns in recent years.

The number of non-business trips (and the overall total) had slowly declined after peaking in 1989–90 because of the economic downturn. On the other hand, business trips followed an upward trend during the recession for two perceived reasons: first, the economy grew generally during the recession, even if growth was low; and secondly, transport and accommodation were cheaper because of airline deregulation and oversupply in the accommodation sector.

Following economic recovery, domestic tourism was expected to grow— non-business trips at a forecast annual growth rate of 1.9 per cent over the six years to 1998–99 and business travel at a slightly lower average annual growth rate of 1.7 per cent. Table 16.1 shows the outlook.

Although the reasons why individuals travel vary widely, it has been found that the total number of trips taken for non-business reasons was related primarily to the level of real household disposable income and the unemployment rate: on average a 1 per cent rise in disposable income could be expected to result in a 0.4 per cent increase in the number of trips taken; and a 10 per cent decline in the unemployment rate (for example, from 8 per cent to 7.2 per cent) could be expected to result in a 0.6 per cent increase in the number of trips taken.

Travel and accommodation costs do not appear to affect the decision to take a trip, though they may cause people to switch destinations, stay in cheaper accommodation or with friends, or take shorter trips. The motivation to travel is strong; the choice of where to travel, where to stay and so on is flexible. It was with these considerations in mind that the non-business growth rate was forecast, as shown in Table 16.2.

Growth in business trips was found to relate to changes in the level of real non-farm gross domestic product (GDP) and the relative cost of travel and accommodation. Thus a 1 per cent increase in GDP can be expected to

Table 16.1   Domestic trips, 1989–90 to 1998–99, in millions

Year	Non-business	Business	Total
1989–90	42.6	7.39	50.0
1990–91	41.3	7.66	49.0
1991–92	40.4	7.92	48.3
1992–93	40.0	7.84	47.8
1993–94	41.3	8.03	49.3
1994–95	42.2	8.15	50.3
1995–96	42.9	8.29	51.2
1996–97	43.4	8.44	51.9
1997–98	44.2	8.60	52.7
1998–99	44.8	8.69	53.5

Sources: *Forecast*, August 1994; BTR — *Domestic Tourism Monitor* for actual figures from 1989–90 to 1992–93; thereafter figures are forecasts

Table 16.2   Non-business trips: forecast assumptions and growth rates

Year	Gross real household disposable income	Unemployment rate	Forecast growth rate
	%*	%	%*
1993–94	2.75	10.50	3.3
1994–95	3.75	9.85	2.2
1995–96	3.10	9.40	1.7
1996–97	2.30	9.10	1.3
1997–98	2.20	8.20	1.7
1998–99	2.00	7.50	1.5

* Percentage change from the preceding year
Sources: *Forecast*, August 1994, Federal Budget Statement, 1994–95; Syntec — Five-year Forecasts; BTR projections

Table 16.3   Business trips: forecast assumptions and growth rates

Year	Real non-farm gross domestic product	Travel and accommodation index	Forecast growth rate
	%*		%*
1993–94	4.00	98.9	2.6
1994–95	3.80	101.1	1.5
1995–96	4.00	103.7	1.6
1996–97	3.80	106.8	1.9
1997–98	3.30	110.2	1.8
1998–99	3.00	114.0	1.1

*Percentage change from the preceeding year
Source: *Forecast*, August 1994, Federal Budget Statement 1994–95; ABARE — *Outlook 94*; BTR projections

lead to a 4 per cent increase in business trips, and a 1 per cent decrease in the relative cost of travel and accommodation can be expected to lead to a 0.8 per cent increase in business trips. This is demonstrated in Table 16.3.

International forecasts

Before the Forecasting Council's technical committee got to work on its own forecasts of international arrivals, it examined the predictions of various organisations of overseas visitors as far ahead as 2000. These had been made before Sydney was awarded the Olympic Games for that year. What it found is illustrated in Table 16.4.

The Council distinguished between forecasts of activity levels and what it considered was the ATC approach of generating marketing goals or targets. The ATC's targets took into consideration a wider range of factors than the other organisations' forecasts, including input by industry and ATC staff. Forecasts are based on models of travel behaviour which incorporate factors such as price, income and recent arrivals.

Table 16.4   Predictions of visitor numbers for 2000

Forecasts:	million
Bureau of Transport and Communications (BTCE)	4.62
Bureau of Tourism Research (BTR)	4.82
Federal Airports Corporation (FAC)	5.01
Qantas Airways	5.70
Economist Intelligence Unit (EIU)	5.90
Targets:	
Australian Tourist Commission (ATC)	6.82

Source: *Forecast*, August 1994

According to the Council, the approaches taken to forecasting by the Bureau of Transport and Communications, Bureau of Tourism Research, Federal Airports Corporation and Qantas were very similar. They generated their forecasts from econometric models in which overseas visitor arrivals were seen as being determined largely by income in the source markets and the price of travelling to Australia relative to other price movements. The Economist Intelligence Unit approach was more complex. Models were first produced to project travel to and within the Far East-Pacific region from each important origin country and then source projections were allocated to different destinations to produce inbound forecasts.

> While forecasts represent an attempt to estimate the likely future given a continuation of past trends and known relationships, targets are usually used to indicate the potential if favourable changes from past practices are made, such as increased marketing efforts or policy changes to make travel easier or cheaper.
>
> Forecasts and targets should be seen as complementary, with their differences indicating the potential gain from policy and other changes.[9]

The Council's approach is to construct econometric models for more than 15 of Australia's major markets. Results from these models will then be augmented by consideration of a range of qualitative factors and then the industry will be asked to comment before the forecasts are finally issued. The idea is that the forecasts will not only reflect what is known about the way markets have performed in the past, but also industry expectations about future developments.

The hope is that investors in general and institutions in particular will understand more about travel and tourism and have more faith in its future as a result of the Council's forecasting work. There is a similar expectation with the Stock Exchange's Tourism and Leisure Index. Taken together, these measures will raise the profile of travel and tourism among investors and give it a solidity it has not had before.

CHAPTER 17

Plans and organisations

ABOUT THIS CHAPTER

What is required for a national plan which will seek to balance marketing and the provision of tourism plant and facilities? First, there must be a rationalisation of Commonwealth Government agencies and then linkages developed between the Commonwealth, States and regions. Partnership Australia provides a model.

Regions are a priority

The Tourism Forecasting Council will turn its attention to regions as a priority, providing forecasts of numbers of visitors, the time they will spend in the area and their expenditure. This is the Big Picture outlook going local and getting close to the Enterprise View. Most travel and tourism businesses are affected by national trends, but few can plan with certainty only on the basis of national forecasts; they have to be localised.

The Big Picture view of regional forecasts is, however, the beginning of national planning. As the forecasts are examined, deficiencies in tourism plant and other product become discernible and priorities emerge, as do marketing imperatives.

Commonwealth tourism agencies

. . . national agencies began to broaden their programs to encompass both sides of the marketing equation: demand and supply. And a new philosophy emerged: to apply to this scattered industry *modern marketing research*

and then *planning*—to balance promotion and plant capacity and to project both programs five to ten years or more into the future.

It is not my intent to suggest the degree to which national tourism
programs should be directed by government or private enterprise or be
under joint control. The important thing is that there should be a coher-
ent national plan, for today and long into the future.

The day of unplanned tourism should now be *yesterday*.[10]

These words were written in 1974, but Australia has not yet heeded them.
The establishment of the Tourism Forecasting Council gives hope that at
last national planning is possible. However, planning to balance promotion
and plant capacity is not possible under the present arrangement
of Commonwealth Government tourism agencies. It will also require the
co-operation of the States and a different attitude towards regions.

The Commonwealth Government at present has four agencies concerned with travel and tourism:

- **The Department of Tourism** Role: to advise the Minister for Tourism
  and to develop and implement policies and programs that encourage
  the tourism industry to take up opportunities for industry development
  and reduce constraints on, and impediments to, industry development.
- **The Australian Tourist Commission** Role: to increase the number of
  visitors to Australia from overseas; to maximise the benefits to Australia
  from overseas visitors; and to ensure that Australia is protected from
  adverse environmental and social impacts of international tourism.
- **The Bureau of Tourism Research** Role: to provide independent,
  accurate, timely and strategically relevant statistics and analyses to the
  tourism industry, to the government and the community at large. The
  Bureau is part-funded by the States and Territories.
- **The Tourism Forecasting Council** Role: to provide tourism-related
  businesses and the government sector with realistic and relevant forecasts so that tourism can develop based on sound investment decisions.[11]

The ATC's role is marketing overseas; that of the Tourism Forecasting
Council is related to the development of tourism plant. The Department of
Tourism seems to cut across everything despite the apparent limitation of its
role: it is even involved in market and product development, which are
marketing functions.[12]

This confusion of agencies, with their different cultures, needs to
be rationalised before effective planning and implementation can be
undertaken.

A single authority

In 1965 the authors of the Harris, Kerr, Forster report, which led to the Commonwealth setting up the Australian Tourist Commission, had this to say:

> The travel and tourist industry, then, should be understood as an over-all industry, involving high degrees of skilled and experienced managements in the operation of its various segments. Because of its many components, it should be regarded as an industry requiring co-ordination, planning and research, and a high level of co-operative action by State and Commonwealth Governments and private enterprise organizations directly engaged in the travel industry.[13]

The authors recommended that:

> *The Commonwealth Government should establish an organization in the form of an authority, board, commission, or corporation for the purpose of co-ordinating the planning and development of the Travel and Tourist Industry of Australia and the promotion of travel from overseas . . .*
>
> The proposed Authority should have two operating divisions:
> (1) *Internal Development Division*, with the necessary staff for research, planning and other co-ordinating activities . . .
> (2) *Overseas Promotion Division* to execute the overseas travel promotion programme and to administer the necessary staff therefor in Australia and abroad.[14]

There is nothing unusual in this approach. The British Tourist Authority, Britain's national tourist organisation, says much the same thing in a different way:

> The Authority's responsibilities are to:
> * promote tourism to Britain from overseas
> * advise Government on tourism matters affecting Britain as a whole
> * encourage the provision and improvement of tourist amenities and facilities in Britain.[15]

The establishment of the Tourism Forecasting Council has seen the beginning of the Commonwealth Government's involvement in the planning of tourism plant development. The high-level Council membership has the right mix of interests and skills to produce effective policies to guide an Australian national tourist organisation which encompasses both marketing and the development of tourism facilities. All necessary functions should be entrusted to a single organisation.

Co-operation with the States

A Tourism Ministers' Council, representing the Commonwealth and States and Territories, has been meeting in Australia since 1959. It has agreed on guidelines detailing responsibilities for the various parties in regard to travel and tourism, and specifically on their roles in overseas promotion. Officials representing government tourist authorities also meet each year.

There have been periods when the spirit of competition which is natural in domestic tourism seemed to be all-pervading, but the current Partnership Australia program provides an example of co-operation which might be carried over into the planning field. Partnership Australia is a co-operative marketing venture aimed at overseas markets. The ATC and all State and Territory tourism organisations are involved. The aims of the program are:

- to provide tourism information to overseas consumers and industry in a way that generates more sales and to extend product distribution in overseas regions.
- develop tourism product for international markets.
- motivate and train the travel industry overseas to sell Australia better.
- improve the efficiency of Australia's tourism marketing effort.[16]

The ATC has the responsibility under the program to develop awareness of and desire to travel to Australia; while the State and Territory tourism authorities, in partnership with the ATC and industry members, focus on tactical marketing linked to specific ATC marketing campaigns.

Members of the industry can have their products listed for a centralised telephone service the ATC has set up for travel agents in a number of important markets. They first approach their State organisation, which checks their products and sends them on to the ATC along with information about their regions.

So regions, States, Territories and the national marketing body all co-operate in a series of linkages which have proved workable. Similar linkages could be established for planning which moves from region to State or Territory to national level, and incorporates the development of tourist facilities and their marketing. Co-operation between the three levels of tourism is the only way the Big Picture and the Enterprise View can progress in harmony and Australia can ensure its growth in travel and tourism is kept in balance.

A need for positive leadership

A prerequisite for success is that the Commonwealth Government should be willing to take a more positive leadership role than in the past and be prepared to work directly with the industry in tourism development through a single agency, perhaps supported by industry.

> Our plans miscarry because they have no aim. When a man does not know what harbour he is making for, no wind is the right wind.[17]

To repeat an earlier quotation: the day of unplanned tourism should be yesterday. As a nation we have wasted a lot of yesterdays. Now, as our tourism grows, the stakes are much higher, too high for wasted opportunities.

NOTES ON SECTION 6

[1] Geoff Burchill, Cairns resort designer and developer, quoted in *Business Review Weekly*, 14 February 1992, p. 21.
[2] *Weekend Australian*, 2–3 April 1994, Property 3.
[3] *The Age*, 4 May 1994, p. 31.
[4] *Weekend Australian*, 24–25 September 1994.
[5] ibid. David Barron, Executive Director of Property with Mercantile Mutual, is quoted.
[6] *Business Review Weekly*, 14 February 1992, p. 21.
[7] It is a curiously constructed document. It says one of its purposes is to provide a 'clear statement of the Commonwealth Government's objectives for the future development of the tourism industry'. But it states no objectives, beyond broad goals relating to economics, the physical and social environments and industry development. It then discusses issues and states strategies, which are again very broad—and, having no objectives to relate to, gives no clear picture of what the Government is about in travel and tourism. Indeed, if the reader tries to work backwards, constructing the objectives from the strategies, a disconcerting picture of dilettantism emerges in some areas (accommodation, for instance, where the strategies relate only to forecasting models and encouraging a more diverse range of tourism accommodation).
[8] *Forecast*, August 1994, p. 18.
[9] *Forecast*, August 1994, p. 8. This part is based on two articles, 'Domestic tourism, first forecasts', pp. 3–6 and 'Understanding international arrival projections', pp. 7–9.
[10] Dan Wallace, Director of Marketing, Canadian Government Office of Tourism, speech to the American Management Associations Conference, New York, February 1974.
[11] The roles of the Department and the Bureau are taken from the Department's 1992–93 Annual Report, the role of the ATC from its 1993 Annual Report and that of the Tourism Forecasting Council from *Forecast*, August 1994.
[12] The product development activities listed in the Department's 1992–93 Annual Report include: rural tourism, marine tourism, cultural tourism, sports tourism, backpacker market, meetings industry. The Annual Report also details a program for the development and marketing of domestic tourism.
[13] Harris, Kerr, Forster & Company and Stanton Robbins & Co., Inc., *Australia's Travel and Tourist Industry*, 1965, p. 65.
[14] ibid, p. 76.
[15] *Selling Britain to the World*, British Tourist Authority Annual Report 1991–92.
[16] *Co-operative Marketing Guide 1994–5*, Australian Tourist Commission.
[17] Lucius Annaeus Seneca (c. 4 BC–AD 65), Roman philosopher and playwright.

Index